YOU'RE MY FA PERSON.

Secrets to staying connected with your adult child
Ruby Peters

Table Of Contents

Chapter 1: How Parent's Influence Affects The Adult Child

There's clear substantiation that parents can and do influence children. There's inversely clear substantiation that children's inheritable makeup affects their behavioral characteristics, and also influences the way they're treated by their parents.

Twin and relinquishment studies give a sound base for estimating the strength of inheritable goods, although heritability estimates for a given particularity vary extensively across samples, and no bone estimate can be considered definitive.

This chapter argues that knowing only the strength of inheritable factors, still, isn't a sufficient base for estimating environmental bones

and indeed, that attempts to do so can underrate parenthood goods. Children's inheritable tendencies and their parents ' child rearing administrations are seen to be nearly simple, and how they serve concertedly to affect children's development are explored.

preface
What are the forces that affect when and how children will change as they grow older? Can development be seen as a progressive process whereby children move toward a specifiable outgrowth or end state that we can call maturity? What conditions determine differences among children in their rates of development or their ultimate issues?
These questions have been at the heart of the importance of the work in experimental psychology since the commencement of the field. In pursuing the answers, the broad forces of nature and nurture, and the interplay between them, have been of central concern.
It has long been clear that there are important maturational time-tables governing experimental change. g. the progression in immaturity from sitting to crawling to standing to walking, or in the accession of language, the transition from rudimentary one-word utterances through intermediate expressions to the product of full, well-formed rulings.
Still, it has been inversely egregious that children are learning numerous effects through their diurnal gests in interacting with the physical and social world, and that what's learned isn't decoded in the genes.
Some of the gests children have are arbitrary — not planned or organized by any outside agency — but some do according to what might be called a socialization timetable. It's then that parenthood has its place.
All societies define certain characteristics that their members are anticipated to retain and certain effects people mustn't do if they're to function adequately as members of their society. Some of these conventions and prohibitions are nearly universal across societies, similar to the demand for parents, or specified parent surrogates, to give productivity and protection to children.
Other norms and values vary greatly from one artistic setting to another. In all societies, training of children occurs, and social controls are in place to ensure that children are mingled — that is, brought up in such a way that each new generation acquires the specified patterns of beliefs and actions. Of course, societies do

2

change, either sluggishly or fleetly, so the cross-generational transmission is by no means absolute.

A new generation may need to acclimatize to conditions that the parent generation didn't face. And the transmission of values, indeed when they continue to be applicable for succeeding generations, isn't always successful. Some children in every cohort may be seen to be deficiently mingled by the criteria that the society applies.

Not all socialization occurs in nonage. People are mingled into the customs and norms of an occupational culture when they take up an entry- position job. Socialization and resocialization do when grown-ups enter into new life places(e.g. marriage, parenting). In considering the part of parents, still, we're substantially concerned with nonage socialization.

Some of the socialization that occurs throughout nonage is in a sense anticipated, in that it functions to prepare children for adoption to a fairly wide range of living places and the children of the colorful surrounding will encounter as they grow older. But nonage socialization also concerns the training of children in modes of geste that are respectable for the stage of nonage they presently enthrall.

Societies set different norms for people at different stages of their life cycle, and some conditions impede especially large in nonage. These include conditions for children to misbehave with adult demands, to avoid prickly grown-ups or dismembering their conditioning, to accept age-applicable responsibility, and to serve as affable, collaborative family members.

In ultramodern societies, there are at least three major environments in which nonage socialization takes place: families, peer groups, and out-of-home surroundings similar to academy classrooms or day-care centers in which the diurnal guests of children are structured and overseen by grown-ups.

The enormous body of literature on nonage socialization has explosively emphasized the part of parents. This emphasis has a long and deep tradition. The idea that " as the branch is fraudulent, so grows the tree " can be traced at least as far back as Greek and Biblical times —(presumably before), and in utmost societies parents are the bones assigned primary responsibility for " bending " the children in desirable directions, by supervising, tutoring, and chastising them as they grow up.

Beforehand nonage in particular has long been allowed to be a period in the life cycle when humans are especially plastic — a time when children are especially open to social influences on characteristics they will carry with them long after they've left their family of origin. Effects are especially vulnerable to influence in the first 5 – 7 times of children's lives including the language they speak, their food preferences, their religious beliefs, and certain continuing personality traits.

In the twentieth century, hypotheticals about the significance of within-family nonage socialization have been part of the fabric of mainstream cerebral propositions. From roughly the 1920s through the 1960s, behaviorist literacy propositions held sway, emphasizing the " blank slate " status of babies and the power of grown-ups to educate youthful children, for good or ill, what they must learn.

Parents, of course, were seen as the most available preceptors, and the bones responsible for carrying out the training of their children. The physiological drive countries(hunger, fatigue) with which children are constitutionally endowed weren't ignored in the literacy propositions of the time, so there was some blending of nature and nurture, but the major emphasis was on the control of literacy processes exercised by environmental inputs.

Psychoanalytic propositions of this period emphasized the significance of early in-family experience in determining posterior inner conflicts, defense mechanisms, and internalization of values. In more recent decades, as the cognitive revolution took hold and literacy proposition(as it affiliated to socialization) was reformulated as cognitive social literacy proposition, the active part of children as actors in their socialization was decreasingly stressed.

Presently, there's adding emphasis on the part of parents ' and children's collective comprehension and understanding of each other's dispositions and intentions as determiners of their influence upon one another. But none of these theoretical shifts has greatly affected the underpinning supposition that parents have an important impact on the characteristics children develop and the directions their lives take.

The child development exploration literature has continued to include a wide range of studies on similar effects as(a) domestic threat factors(i.e. aspects of the family performing that are related to the posterior development of materializing or internalizing diseases in children);(b) social conditions that affect similar parenthood practices as to how well parents are suitable to cover their children, or how warm and responsive they are; and(c) parenthood actions as intercessors of the connection between societal threat factors(e.g. poverty or dangerous neighborhoods) and children's adaptation.

In recent decades, there has been a countervailing ground swell of exploration and theorizing about nature — the inheritable talent of parents and children — as playing an important influence on the characteristics that children develop.

Of course, for numerous decades, abecedarian psychology handbooks have carried tables comparing identical and brotherly halves concerning their degree of similarity in IQ or other traits. Studies of espoused children were also extensively reported numerous times agone , and consequences were routinely drawn from both binary and relinquishment studies concerning the significance of inheritable factors in development.

Still, numerous times, allowing remained largely compartmentalized, and compendiums continued to believe in both the significance of inheritable factors and the significance of socialization factors as though they were in no way inharmonious. In recent times, still, there have been more sophisticated work in geste genetics, and pertinacious voices are claiming that the findings from this work are indeed inharmonious with numerous extensively-held views about the power of within-family socialization.

These dispatches from geste genetics have been picked up and synthesized with other misgivings about the sins of socialization exploration into a more broad-based attack on traditional hypotheticals concerning parenthood and its goods.

Rowe's book, The Limits of Family Influence(1994), stated the case explosively, and Harris's more popular book The Nurture Assumption(1998) attracted a flurry of media attention to the issues. These authors have drawn together the findings from some well-known studies of parenthood goods and findings from geste genetics to make the following claims

1.

The connections that studies have set up between the way parents deal with their children and how the children turn out are relatively

5

weak and have proved delicate to replicate. When parents' ' goods are set up, they tend to be goods on the way children are born at home and the connections they develop with their parents. There's little carry-over from at-home guests to the way children serve in out-of-home surrounds
2.

When studies do establish connections between parenthood and children's attributes, these are correlational findings. An illustration is Baumrind's early finding — now extensively replicated — that the children of parents who are both responsive and firm tend to be more competent and collaborative than children of parents who are either authoritarian or permissive(Baumrind & Black 1967).

Similar findings have traditionally been interpreted as showing that authoritative parenthood has salutary goods on children, ignoring the possibility that the unproductive connection may run the other way — i.e. that competent, collaborative children may make it easier for their parents to be firm and responsive. The critics argue, that parents geste is mainly driven by the geste of children, and important if not utmost of the parent/ child correlation can be reckoned for by the child's inheritable tendencies.

3.

Maternal influence has been emphasized at the expense of sources of influence that have great — or maybe lesser — significance in shaping children's development. Two kinds of influence that critics argue have been underemphasized are inheritable tendencies and the influence of peers.

In the popular media, these reviews have been condensed into the oversimplified communication " Parents don't matter " or " matter veritably little " — news mouthfuls that, on their face, have little relation to reality as it's endured daily in family life. frequently, reports in the popular media don't reflect what the cited authors said.

For illustration, late in her book, Harris(1998) says she believes parents can foster the development of specific bents(e.g. by furnishing music assignments) and can impact similar effects as children's rest time conditioning, their food preferences, their religious beliefs and practices, and the accession of knowledge and chops and preferences that will contribute to their ultimate choice of a profession.

Yet, the burden of her book is to downplay similar influences and stress the felicitations in which parents aren't influential. Rowe says " ... parents in utmost working to professional-class families may have little influence on what traits their children may ultimately develop as grown-ups. "(19947). His use of the word " may " doesn't greatly soften the import of his communication. He goes on to say that he doubts whether any undesirable particularity displayed by a child can be significantly modified by anything a parent does. Scarr(1992) expresses an also skeptical view about the possible goods of interventions.

Similar views, of course, when picked up and simplified in the popular press, can have serious counter accusations for public programs concerning whether to invest in remedial or probative programs for children and families

These reviews constitute serious sweats to present a point of view that's easily different from the traditional emphasis on the significance of parenthood. They cite large bodies of data and have attracted the support of largely estimable psychologists. They earn to be taken seriously.

Nevertheless, I believe that they're out of date concerning both the inheritable studies and the parenthood-goods studies they cite and that they seriously misinterpret the material body of exploration.

How Strong is the Connection Between Parent and Child Actions?

As noted over, critics charge that practitioners of traditional socialization studies have exaggerated the significance of parenthood in children's lives — that in fact, the effect sizes reported in numerous extensively- cited studies are relatively small. Indeed, reviews of exploration done before themed-1980s did show weak correlations between parenthood processes and children's characteristics(e.g. Maccoby & Martin 1983).

Also, numerous studies have come up with further robust findings, no distrustfulness reflecting advancements in how parent and child characteristics are assessed. Leading experimenters no longer calculated on a single measure, similar to a parent or child interview or a parent or child tone-report scale, as a measure of parent or child attributes.

Rather information is obtained from multiple sources — from parents, children, preceptors, academy records, occasionally from children's peers and police records as well — and importantly, from direct observation of parent-child relations and of children in out-of-home settings. When several measures similar to these are added up, associations between parent attributes and children's geste can be relatively substantial. Parents have generally reckoned for 20 to 50 of the friction in child issues(Conger & Elder 1994, Reiss et al 1995).

Exceptionally robust connections are reported in the recent large-scale study of adolescents in norway - disassociated and step-families, Hetherington and associates(Hetherington et al 1999). Using compound scores for both parenthood styles and children's attributes, report a concurrent measure of0.76 between mater ' " authoritative parenthood " and adolescents ' " social responsibility "(the measure for fathers is 0.49).

Maternal negativity has veritably strong connections for both parents with adolescents ' depression and internalizing geste . 1 Patterson and associates have also set up substantial correlations between maternal characteristics(e.g. correctional practices and monitoring) and children's asocial geste. They're suitable to show connections between maternal actions and the children's negative, coercive geste both at home and in out-of-home surroundings.

Concurrent correlations are generally vastly larger than prophetic bones . Longitudinal studies present the occasion to examine the connections, if any, between child-rearing styles at one point in time and posterior attributes of the child.

The strength of the connections that have been set up depends on numerous effects, such as what " packages' ' or clusters of parent and child variables are considered, the way they're measured, the length of time between prophetic and outgrowth measures, and whether background variables are statistically controlled. Many exemplifications will illustrate the range of findings.

Kochanska 1997b94 has been suitable to show that aspects of early parenthood account for a significant but moderate(Beta measure 0.29, F9.96) portion of the friction in youthful children's tone-regulation and internalization assessed a time later.

Pettit and associates(1997908) set up some — but smaller and weaker — prophetic connections between parenthood as assessed in the morning of kindergarten time and children's adaptation and academic performance seven times later, in the sixth grade. The strong prophetic power of family commerce processes over much longer periods has been set up in longitudinal studies of asocial geste.

In current socialization studies, simple first-order correlations between parenthood characteristics and child issues are infrequently reckoned on. Indeed, occasionally they aren't reported. rather, multivariate analyses are used to probe similar questions as to whether a given aspect of parenthood has different goods on different kinds of children or in families living in different circumstances; or whether different aspects of parenthood have independent, cumulative goods, whether they're exchangeable, or whether they interact so that the goods of one depending on the position of another.

In longitudinal work, the original position of a child's specific at time 1 is occasionally statistically controlled to determine whether a time- 1 parent trait is associated with the posterior change in the child's geste .

As an illustration, Patterson & Bank(1989) studied families when their sons were in grade academy, and again when the boys were adolescents.

They established that changes in parenthood during these times were explosively related to the chances of a boy being arrested for tardy conditioning in nonage, indeed after the boy's anti-social tendencies at grade- academy age was controlled. We see, also, that a variety of questions are being asked in current and recent exploration — questions to which simple parent/ child correlations, either concurrent or time-lagged, won't give answers.

A word should be said, too, about how large a correlation between some aspect of parenthood and a child's outgrowth is needed for the relationship to be considered important or meaningful. Along with the rest of the cerebral discipline, experimental psychologists are presently turning down from reporting the issues of studies primarily(or only) in terms of significant situations(p values) that indicate the degree of departure from the null thesis. rather, results are beginning to be reported in terms of effect sizes.

For purposes of policy opinions in the medical arena, correlations as small as0.03 between the use of a drug and reduction of complaints have been considered strong enough to justify the FDA blessing of the medicine(Rosenthal 1999). The significance of medical intervention can be estimated in terms of similar issues as the number of heart attacks prevented or the number of people for whom an enervating, habitual complaint can be arrested or reversed. In history, correlations in the 0.20 s or0.30 s between aspects of family functioning and children's issues have frequently been dismissed as inconsequential.

But when restarted into the number of children who are at threat, for illustration, for failing in academia or getting tardy or seriously depressed, prophetic portions of this magnitude can be seen as by no means trivial. From the viewpoint of social policy, the issue becomes one of how important significance a society attaches to social/ behavioral issues, as compared with medical bones. This is a matter of values, not statistics.

Studies continue to vary vastly concerning the size of first-order correlations between parent and child characteristics. easily, a given parent may have different goods on different children, depending on similar effects as age, coitus, disposition, and distinctive previous experiences. However, adding up data across a whole sample of children will wash out parent/ child goods — goods that might be relatively robust within sub-groups of children, If similar discriminational goods live.

It isn't possible to arrive at any general rule as to when dividing by groups will increase or drop a parent-child correlation. That will depend on the experimenter's theoretical and empirical skill in relating what the material groupings might be. The use of further sophisticated statistical styles has contributed significantly to the capability of present-day experimenters to identify parenthood goods within the matrix of other factors with which they frequently vary.

Not only have styles of assessment been better, but current socialization exploration includes a broader array of parenthood attributes and focuses on a set of parenthood processes that weren't so easily delineated at times once.

One aspect of maternal skill that has surfaced in several recent studies as related to children's well-being is ménage association; another concerns the capability of some parents to develop a complementary form of commerce with their children(e.g. participating in positive effect, collective responsibility).

Studies of the prophetic power of parent-child negotiation in early nonage have yielded relatively robust parenthood goods. These exemplifications illustrate how the field of the family- impact studies has been growing in abstract as well as methodological strength. Nonetheless, we must be conformed to the fact that there are important aspects of parenthood that will never be revealed in studies that, by necessity, try to synopsize maternal characteristics into measurable clusters or traits.

There are the memorable little socialization moments when the members of a parent/ child duo are, for some reason, especially attuned to one another — when the child, maybe by having encountered a new and salient issue, is ready to both explain and hear.

At such a moment, the parent may do or say a commodity that makes a deep print and can have a continuing influence. Again, a broken pledge or a revealed deception may break the prevailing relationship of trust between the two, changing the nature of the influence that's possible between them. Similar moments are unique to a duo and may not be captured in socialization studies, indeed though our mindfulness of them is stressed in lives, autobiographies, and fabrication.

I don't want to claim too much importance for the strength of maternal influence in children's lives. Critics are right in pointing out that we've overemphasized these influences at the expense of other kinds of environmental influences. To what extent early nonage is a time of especially great malleability, during which environmental inputs will be more likely to have a continuing influence than inputs latterly in life is an open question. presumably, the answer will vary, depending on what sphere of children's development we're talking about. (See for illustration,

Neville's finding(Neville 1995) that the openness to impact by early experience differs between the semantic and syntactic language systems). Because parents are generally the ones who spend the utmost time with youthful children over extended ages of time, these questions of changing malleability do matter in our sweats to understand the maternal realm of influence.

Still, parents are far from the only source of influence on children, and as children grow older, they're more and more subject to the influence of peers, seminaries, preceptors, and TV. Also, there are the arbitrary events — a serious illness or accident, an unanticipated success, a domestic move, an environmental catastrophe — that can alter the line of a child's life in ways that have little to do with parenthood.

Of course, when we do see robust correlations between parent and child attributes, the question of the direction of goods arises formally.

In making their argument that we may be seeing child-to-parent goods rather than the rear, critics have reckoned heavily on the findings of geste genetics 2, especially on studies of halves and espoused children. They've also reckoned on these findings to suggest that nonparental aspects of a child's terrain have lesser weight than maternal inputs in determining how a child will develop.

The Challenge from Behavior Genetics

Some of the major findings of geste

genetics are important and bear scholars of socialization to reevaluate some of their hypotheticals. numerous of these findings are well known, and I don't epitomize them in any detail then, but concentrate on the main lines of argument that bear on the issue of parenthood goods.

The Focus on Variation

Behavior geneticists seek to understand the sources of variation in some mortal particularity or characteristic. Their approach is to be distinguished from that of evolutionary psychologists, who seek to understand the inherited underpinnings of characteristics that are fairly invariant across a species.

There are important goods of both genes and terrain that are overlooked in studies that concentrate on the variation of a characteristic within a given population. A mortal characteristic similar to being born with two eyes is entirely inheritable, yet its heritability would be reckoned as zero in a twin or relinquishment study since it's a characteristic that doesn't vary within the population studied.

Also, there may be an environmental factor that affects the mean position of a characteristic — caregiving or lowering all scores to an analogous degree — without greatly disturbing the rank- order of individualities on the characteristic.

Therefore, relinquishment studies have set up that the correlation of espoused children's masterships with those of their natural parents can remain substantial, while at the same time the average Command of the espoused children are more advanced than that of their natural parents, as though children admit a Command perk from being espoused into fairly stable, middle- class homes, while nonetheless continuing to differ from each other according to their inheritable talent. In a study of French children espoused at about the age of 5, it was set up that the quantum of increase in their masterships(assessed again in nonage) was vastly lesser for children espoused into rich, well-educated families than for those espoused into depressed homes.

Temporal trends illustrate the same point. The " Flynn effect "(Flynn 1987, 1999) — the substantial, monotonic rise in mean Command scores over numerous decades in Western bucolic countries — is well known.

There has been a substantial rise in the rates of smoking among American women in the last several decades, and the rates of drinking alcohol dropped during prohibition. These changes, of course, have passed during ages of time that are much too short to reflect any inheritable changes and they've passed even though heritability estimates for IQ, drinking, and smoking have remained relatively stable over the same time periods during which the average situations were changing.

An analogous miracle is seen in some migration studies, in which alternate-generation emigrants are on average relatively different from their foreign-born grandparents, indeed on largely inheritable traits similar to height.

The recrimination of these marvels for parenthood goods is this: There may have been temporal changes in parenthood — touched off maybe by similar effects as changes in family structure or overall profitable position — that have had wide goods on children without affecting heritability estimates for the outgrowth characteristics being affected.

These important environmental goods are missed in the estimates of E(terrain) deduced from geste genetics studies of halves and espoused children. Another way of putting this point is to note that the high heritability of a particularity doesn't indicate that it isn't also subject to the influence of environmental factors, or that it can not be changed by differences in environmental conditions.

It's for this reason that, when comparing group means(by race, coitus, or socioeconomic status) it isn't licit to interpret any group differences in terms of estimates of inheritable or environmental goods deduced from quantitative Jeste
 inheritable studies.

 Experimental Interventions with Parents If large-scale environmental events can change the mean situations of a character without greatly changing the rank-order of individualities, it follows that experimental interventions might do the same.

It's delicate to change factual parenthood practices through parent-training programs, and also to document that program-convinced changes in parenthood change the mean situations of children's characteristics. similar programs must be longitudinal, of course, and must have an undressed control group for comparison.

Studies that intermediate with the parents but don't contemporaneously treat the children, and that have the arbitrary assignment of families to treatment or control groups, are understandably rare, but several have easily shown that when treatment is suitable to change maternal geste toward children in specified ways, the geste of children changes similarly suitable to show that it was indeed the reduction of parent-to-child coercive geste , brought about by a parent-training intervention with an aimlessly assigned experimental group, that produced declining situations of asocial geste in a group of aggressive children.

An intervention program that changes the mean of a group of parents(and accordingly, of their children's geste as well) may or may not change the original rank order of the children. Experimenters generally find that some parents are told further than others by intervention, and some children are affected further than others by advancements in maternal correctional or monitoring practices.

These discriminational goods might either increase or drop the range of outgrowth scores in the treatment group, depending on whether it was the originally more- performing or inadequately-performing families who were most affected by the intervention. still, expanding or shrinking the range of outgrowth scores doesn't inescapably change the original rank- order.

The point then is that changes in a mean can be independent of any changes in rank order. Therefore, changes in a mean can easily demonstrate an environmental effect, relatively piecemeal from any correlational information(grounded on rank orders of individualities) that might be used to cipher inheritable or environmental goods in an inheritable analysis. The environmental goods revealed by the mean change would go undetected in a correlational analysis.

The Claim for Substantial inheritable goods In traditional geste

Inheritable exploration, data from studies of halves and espoused children are used to cipher heritability estimates(h2), which are interpreted as estimates of the proportion of friction reckoned for by inheritable factors. numerous similar studies have yielded substantial heritability estimates. Identical halves have been set up to be more analogous to each other than are same- coitus brotherly halves concerning a wide range of characteristics, including vulnerability to certain conditions, intelligence, disposition, and several personality characteristics.

The conclusion is that this must be due to their lesser inheritable similarity because the important aspects of their surroundings — parenthood entered, neighborhood, presence of a same-age, same-coitus stock — are presumably inversely analogous for the two kinds of binary dyads. espoused children have been set up to be more analogous to their natural parents than to their consanguineous parents concerning a named set of characteristics for which experimenters have been suitable to gain measures from both natural and consanguineous parents.

In a general sense, the geste geneticists have made their case. Children's inheritable bents do easily affect how individualities will develop — in comparison to other children — to a much lesser extent than was allowed to be the case during the times of the ascendance of underpinning learning propositions and psychodynamic propositions(the middle decades of the twentieth century.)

How substantial is this inheritable donation?

Critics have argued that estimates deduced from binary studies overrate the inheritable donation to a particularity because identical halves have further analogous surroundings than do same-coitus brotherly halves. Identical halves(compared with fraternals) are treated more also by their parents, spend further time together(and hence constitute a lesser proportion of each other's social terrain), and more frequently partake in the same musketeers.

presumably, the lesser similarity in the surroundings of identical halves isn't sufficiently strong to negate the findings on inheritable goods, but it does weaken them. It probably helps to regard the fact that heritability estimates are generally larger in binary studies than in relinquishment studies.

Of course, the inheritable donation might be anticipated to be lesser for some mortal attributes than others. It appears to be more substantial for measures of intellectual capacities than for social or personality attributes.

Still, it's delicate to establish a dependable, generalizable estimate for any given particularity. For one thing, estimates vary depending on the source of information for measuring a particularity. When children's characteristics are assessed through parents ' conditions, heritability estimates are frequently vastly more advanced than when assessments are deduced from behavioral compliances of the children, from children's tone- reports, or from school teacher conditions.

It appears that parents see their children as further different from one another than other sources of information find them to be(a discrepancy effect). In a recent review of studies on the heritability of aggressive geste , Cadoret and associates(Cadoret et al 1997) report a veritably wide range of heritability portions,(from near zero to over.70), with the advanced numbers coming from studies using parent report measures, and the lower bones
from experimental studies.

Miles & Carey(1997), in a meta-analysis of 24 binary and relinquishment studies, report mainly lesser values for h2 grounded on parent reports than for those grounded on adolescent tone-reports.

Especially important is the fact that the size of a heritability measure depends greatly on the range of both inherited and environmental factors in the population being studied.

Estimates of the heritability of a given particularity can change vastly when a new estimate is grounded on a culturally different population, or especially when a new estimate includes families from a wider range of mores and socioeconomic situations.

All this means that while the fact of an inheritable donation to mortal variability isn't in mistrustfulness, the size of this donation is indeterminate for any given particularity. More specifically, the size of a heritability estimate can not be generalized from the specific population — in its specific terrain — assessed with the specific set of measures used in a given study.

It's delicate to attune findings similar to these with the claim that the aspects of family surroundings that are participated by siblings don't affect their development. An egregious possibility is that while the family terrain does affect each child, its goods are different for different children. There presumably was an implied supposition, in traditional socialization work, that the goods of participating surroundings would be to make siblings analogous to one another.

What the geste geneticists are telling us is that any influences of domestic circumstances — similar as maternal illness or health, profitable substance or adversity, good or poor parenthood — frequently function to make siblings different rather than analogous. It's possible that a dysfunctional family terrain may have goods on both members of a stock brace, but that the goods aren't similar to make siblings more likewise, but indeed might serve to make them more different.

We know from Elder's work on goods of the Great Depression(Elder 1974) that when a father loses his job, the goods on the child will depend on the age and coitus of the child at the time that this stressful event occurs. Indeed for same-coitus halves, we can imagine that if they were adolescents at the time, one might reply to a father's job loss by going out to get an after-academy job to help support the family while the other might part himself from the family and spend further time " hanging out " with musketeers. Both children would be affected by the change in the family terrain, but else.

Any domestic or maternal factors that serve to make siblings different rather than analogous to one another are assigned, in geste genetics, to the sole rather than the participating environmental element when calculating environmental goods. geste geneticists have noway said that estimates of sole surroundings didn't include parent goods, but they argue that if parenthood does have goods it must take one of two forms parents must be treating different children in their families else(or furnishing different surroundings for them), or different children in the same family who are exposed to analogous parenthood must reply to the same maternal inputs else.

A considerable body of recent work has riveted on the question, What's it that makes siblings different from one another? . In these studies, substantiation is presented that siblings tend to join different peer groups and that siblings have vastly different guests within the environment of the stock relationship itself. The question of how else they're treated by their parents remains open. Studies done during a single period frequently show that two siblings are treated else by their parents.

Still, in a longitudinal study Dunn set up that parents were fairly harmonious in how they treated children at a specific age. That is, an alternate child, when reaching the age of four, is treated in an analogous way to the way his/ her aged stock was treated at that age, indeed though the aged stock may now be entering a different treatment.

Therefore, throughout the " growing up " times, different children in the same family entered similar treatment. This fact, of course, would be missed in any study that didn't look for it longitudinally; the extent of discriminational treatment is likely to be overrated in cross-sectional studies(except in the case of halves). Whether or not children are treated else over the whole span of nonage, there's reason to believe that children's comprehension of how else they're treated may be of considerable significance in children's development, so concurrent differences are important in their own right.

In general, the disquisition of siblings ' sole surroundings has been a productive and instructional enterprise. We now know that the surroundings of children growing up in the same family can indeed be different.

But this doesn't break the problem of how to interpret aspects of the terrain that are truly participating, similar as a maternal illness, family income, parents ' education, or the neighborhood where the family lives — factors that have an impact indeed when they serve to make siblings different rather than likewise.

As noted over, geste geneticists tend to conclude that, since it's clear that these aspects of terrain truly participated, they mustn't be having an effect because Es goods are negligible.

So frequently, we've assumed that the crucial influences on children's development involve their parents ' personality and age, the quality of their parents ' marriage relationship, children's educational background, the neighborhood in which they grow up, and their parents ' station to academy or to discipline. Yet to the extent that these influences participate, they can not regard the differences we observe in children's issues .

On the negative, it seems presumptive that these participating factors may indeed have imported goods that don't show up in calculations of participated environmental goods because of the demand that only an environmental factor that makes siblings more analogous can be called " participated. "

A geste geneticist might say about the effect of a participating environmental factor that makes siblings different, " Oh, but we're calling those sole goods. " But to call an environmental input sole indeed though it's endured by all children in a family(e.g. a father's job- loss, a mama's depression, a move to a better neighborhood) is an unfortunate deformation of the simple meaning of the word " participated. " We could see this as only a trivial matter of language choice, but it can lead to serious misconstructions of geste

geneticists ' findings. By description, they've ruled out the possibility that a truly participating aspect of the terrain could have a significant effect on at least one child when the goods on different children aren't the same.

When we deal with a participated environmental factor that impacts different children in the family else, it could be argued — and geste geneticists do argue — that the effect stems from the fact that some children are more genetically vulnerable to an environmental event than others. In the usual calculations of heritability, such an effect would also be assigned to the G element of the equation, rather than to the environmental bone .

Surely, it's inversely presumptive that both G and E are important then. threat factors, similar to poverty, a father's severance, or a mama's depression, are indeed environmental conditions that are participated by all the children in a family. In large population studies, they will correctly crop as hurting children, indeed though some children are more vulnerable to them than others. In the extreme case, we could imagine that in every two-child family, one of the children would show the injurious goods of poverty and the other would not(maybe because of inheritable differences between them).

Across numerous families, there would be a veritably important effect of poverty and it would be correctly linked as a strong threat factor, indeed though the participated terrain effect would be reckoned at zero. The egregious peril then's that low estimates for Es can be interpreted as meaning that family environmental conditions that children share don't have an impact on their development, whereas the contrary can be true, and frequently is.

The findings from geste genetics on participating and sole surroundings have profound counter accusations for the way we suppose about the child- parenting practices and their goods. For one thing, they concentrate attention on stock differences. This is a commodity that traditional exploration of a child- parenting — nearly always involving only one child per family — did not deal with. It should be noted that there's nothing about the findings of these traditional studies that are abrogated by their having studied only one child. The connections linked between the maternal inputs to this child and the child's characteristics can be dependable, replicable bones

, indeed though if we had studied a different parent-child brace in the same family we might have gotten a different constellation of parenthood and issues. The picture arising from adding up data across a set of one-child cases is valid as well, though the findings are surely downgraded by the within-family stock variation. Still, we get a less differentiated picture than the bone that emerges from the study of siblings.

Family systems proponents have advised us to " niche- picking " by different children in a family — the trouble of children finding distinctive places. Evolutionary proponents have argued that there's natural competition among siblings for maternal attention and other coffers handled by parents.

In short, there's reason to believe that there are forces motivating children to separate themselves from their siblings, and these may annul, or transfigure, the goods of maternal inputs that might otherwise serve to make them the same. Of course, some of the isolation between siblings can come directly from discriminatory treatment by the parents, or it can stem from discriminational responses by different children to the same material inputs.

The dissimilitude of siblings continues to be a commodity we don't completely understand. It has been interpreted to mean that aspects of terrain in which siblings partake — quantum of inter-parental conflict, good or poor neighborhoods, poverty or influx, the position of maternal education or the " artistic " position of the home terrain, ménage association or disorganization, the quantum of good humor characterizing the family atmosphere — all these effects must have veritably little influence on children's development.

This interpretation flies in the face of the large body of exploration on threat factors, which constantly finds strong connections between these aspects of family functioning and children's issues. I argue that the threat-factor findings are indeed valid, but that they need not have the same goods on all children in a family nor function to make siblings more likewise. It begins to feel likely that there are strong factors pushing siblings toward isolation from one another, including maybe competition for maternal attention or other coffers, " niche selecting, " counter identification, and discriminational comprehensions of the stock relationship on the part of the actors in it. similar factors could serve as counter forces, working against maternal inputs that might else make siblings more likewise. But this is enterprise. important remains to be learned about this complex matter.

Numerous factors other than parents ' conduct impact how children grow and develop. As children grow beyond preschool times, they're exposed more and more to other adult socialization agents(preceptors, trainers) and, of course, to individual musketeers and larger peer groups. Within the matrix of factors that affect children's development, it's clear that parenthood goods are real, though they frequently combine with inheritable goods in impacting an outgrowth.

Along with numerous other scholars of these marvels, I suggest that we give up the trouble to partition the unproductive factors impacting children's development into two separate " nature " and " nurture " factors and that we hesitate from asking ourselves which is more important. The two are inextricably interwoven all along the pathway from birth to maturity. So be it. Let us not underrate moreover, but concentrate on how they serve concertedly.

What could affect the child?
It's a question we've presumably all asked ourselves after a particularly rough day " Am I a bad parent? "

It's easy to feel like your parenthood chops are below par in a moment when nothing seems to be going your way, and you've exhausted your tolerance fully.

But the fact that you're concerned about whether you're making the right parenthood choices is a good sign that you're not, in fact, a bad parent.

Occasionally it can feel like every choice we're making is monumental and every mistake significant. We worry about the long-term good of our choices, especially when it comes to negative relations with our children.

We stress over whether we were too harsh when we yelled at them before or if we could have handled that hissy
more, or whether we doled out the applicable consequences.

But every parent has those moments where they lose their cool. We've all made less-than-astral parenthood choices in a moment of frustration or confusion.

That's why we asked two internal health experts to partake tips on how to spot the signs of what we'll call " bad parenthood " and the effect it may have on a child — to help clarify what's worth fussing about.

We've also got some tips on fastening on the positive when it comes to parenthood — because when we're in the fosses, it's oh-so-easy to dwell on the negative.

What's bad parenthood?
Some effects are generally considered " bad " by anyone.

Physical abuse, neglect, emotional abuse, and sexual abuse are the most serious and dangerous geste traits that utmost of us equate with bad parenthood. These are effects that should be incontinently addressed with professional help.

But beyond child abuse and neglect, there are also effects that parents may do or say that can, indeed unintentionally, lead to adverse issues for a child. Feeling whether you're doing those effects can help you to feel better about your parenthood.

Taking an honest assessment of your parenthood style isn't always an easy task. That's why it's important to first separate the geste
from the person.

Calling yourself or someone differently a " bad parent " isn't a commodity to jump to the ground on a difference in beliefs or parenthood style. It's also important to feel there's a difference between having a bad moment and being a bad parent.

Losing your temper every formerly in a while isn't the same as telling your child, " I 'm smart, and you 're dumb " or " I'm right, you're awry, and there's nothing you can do about it. "

23

Although some people differ on what's " good " or " bad " parenthood, utmost parents have both positive and negative parenthood traits.

What are the signs of bad parenthood?
It's easy to see lower than desirable parenthood actions when you consider the axes.

Over or under involvement
On one end, you have the uninvolved parent who's disregardful and fails to respond to their child's requirements beyond the basics of the sanctum, food, and apparel.

While not as damaging as a disregardful style, an over-involved parent(aka copter parent) can also beget further detriment than good by taking control of opinions and doing too important for their child, hindering them from learning by doing.

Little or no discipline
According to Sharron Frederick, LCSW, a psychotherapist at Clarity Health results, children who have little or no discipline are left to fend for themselves, which can affect injuries and also creates a child who doesn't understand boundaries.

" Children look to parents to define what boundaries are and the consequences that can do if the child crosses the boundaries, " she says.

Strict or rigid discipline
Unlike parents who apply little to no discipline, Frederick says parents who exercise strict or rigid discipline(aka authoritarian parenthood) don't allow their child to explore their world, which frequently leads to a child who becomes fearful and anxious or rebellious.

Withdrawing affection and attention

" Ignoring a child is telling them that your love is tentative, " says Frederick. Withdrawing affection because a child doesn't do what they're told causes analogous detriment.

" These types of actions can cause a child to have low tone- regard and low confidence, which can affect a child not expressing their wants and requirements, " she says.

Over time, Frederick says this can lead to codependency, in which the child will acclimatize to how they feel a person wants them to act. " numerous times, this can lead to connections that are vituperative, " she adds.

smirching
Whether in public or private, children who are continually lowered can develop issues with perfection and a fear of failure. This can lead to depression or anxiety.

What are the goods of bad parenthood?
Children without positive parenthood are more at threat of their relationship troubles, depression, anxiety, and aggression, among other negative issues.

The below goods are the result of ongoing patterns of negative geste . That time you yelled at your toddler for breaking your favorite coffee mug isn't the same as a harmonious pattern of a review or physical violence.
Negative Tone- perception
A parenthood misstep that can have continuing consequences is the overuse of negative markers and smirching.

Harmonious use of negative markers similar to name-calling deeply impacts a child's sense of tone and contributes to long-standing negative tone- narratives and tone- fulfilling prognostics.

Shame is an important and paralyzing emotion that becomes deeply bedded in the psyche and sense of tone. Given its strength, numerous people, including parents, engender it to discourage negative geste or motivate toward positive actions.

Still, when smirching and negative labeling come a common tactic, Dorfman says children also begin to internalize and embody these negative dispatches.

They learn to speak to themselves the way they've been spoken to — immortalizing negative passions and getting roughly tone-critical.

Long term, people with negative tone- comprehensions frequently seek connections that will support the dispatches they're habituated to hail.

Control issues and rebellion
Children who witness exorbitantly rigid or strict discipline can have issues with control of others, compulsive- obsessive complaints, and other anxious actions, together with the mindset that the world is dangerous, according to Frederick.

On the other end of the diapason is the rebellious child who fights with their parents, breaks the rules, and engages in negative actions.

Emotional and behavioral problems
Harsh parenthood, which includes verbal or physical pitfalls, frequent yelling, and hitting, along with immediate negative consequences for a specific geste , can lead to children having emotional and behavioral issues, similar to aggressiveness and following directions at the academy.

What can you do to stop bad parenthood?
Although negative parenthood actions can put children at threat, it's not the only factor that determines issues.

Indeed parents with a positive style of discipline and commerce can have children who struggle with behavioral or emotional issues. Just like a single bad day doesn't make you a bad parent, doing the stylish you can doesn't mean that your child will norway struggle or have problems. And that's OK.

Parenthood is an ongoing process, and it's frequently challenging. However, it might feel indeed harder, If you've plodded thanks to less-than-ideal exemplifications from your parents. But you can work to overcome the negative dispatches you've been tutored for and make a healthy relationship with your children.

Your parents may not have been good role models, but you can find support and positive stimulants in other parents to produce your parenthood path.

still, a flashback that you're able to make changes, If you find yourself falling into bad parenthood habits more frequently than you'd like.

Revamping your parenthood style can bear tolerance, honesty, and a lot of hard work. The good news is it's no way too late to start. Any positive change you make can affect a better outgrowth for your child. Here are some tips to help you concentrate on the positive.

Hear to your child's studies and passions
We all want to be heard. And although we don't always agree with what others say, we all need someone to hear us.
When it comes to your kiddies, hear their enterprises and frustrations, validate their passions, and explain that they have a right to be angry — but not to act out(like throwing their crayons across the room). rather, give druthers
for them for different feelings.

Give applicable consequences
When using discipline, it's critical to give consequences that educate your child on a positive assignment. Hitting a child teaches them nothing about consequences, and can affect resentment and wrathfulness, together with that child going to the academy and hitting other children.

Rather, use a price map or have them earn time doing commodities they enjoy. When taking a commodity down, don't take it down for a week, rather, take it down for the autumn. Make sure that the consequence is suitable for the geste you're correcting.

Marker the geste , not the child still, ' they should make sure that they're labeling geste , not character, " If parents want to ' label. For illustration, when a child is acting out, remind them that it's the geste of a bully, rather than saying, " You ARE a bully. "

Don't withhold attention
We all get angry with our children, but Frederick says ignoring them only confuses a child. " Explain that you're angry, and although you're angry with them, you still love them, " she explains.

Still, try putting them in time out(1 nanosecond for every age they are) and calm down, collecting your studies and passions, If you need a moment.

Show love and affection
Displaying love and affection means further than just telling your child that you love them. It also comes from supporting and accepting your child, being physically tender, and spending quality time together.

Let them make miscalculations
Life is messy, so let your children explore being creative and making miscalculations, without smirching or censuring. When they make a mistake, ask your child, " What could you have done else? "

Use your miscalculations as an occasion to show them that literacy noway stops and that we can each have our bad days. Admitting when you've made a mistake, apologizing, and trying to ameliorate is good for everyone.

Takeaway
Being a parent is emotionally grueling. It's also a huge responsibility that requires tolerance, thickness, love, compassion, and understanding.

We all have days when we worry about our parenthood choices. We love our youngsters so much, it's natural to only want something stylish for them.

The flashback that you're learning as you go, and every day is a chance to start fresh. With the right tools and with tolerance for our children — and ourselves — we can each choose the parent we want to be.

Also, a flashback that we all need to support — some days more than others. However, seek help, and guidance, If you're feeling stretched or exorbitantly stressed.

Parenthood is the hardest job in the world. Hang in there — you've got this!

Negative Influence Of Parents On Children

The influence of parenthood on children is huge and impacts how children conduct themselves. For illustration, maintaining an affable atmosphere at home could help nurture a confident child. On the other hand, a child who's anxious and nervous all the time may frequently be exposed to their parent's outrageous actions.

Hence it's important to understand that your life practices and controversies with your mate could largely impact your child's overall development and outlook towards connections in life. Altogether, positive parenthood and parenting could appreciatively impact and hoist a child's life, while bad parenthood can affect a child's regard, internal health, and social life. Read this post to explore the important aspects and consequences of positive and negative parenthood on children.

Negative Influence Of Parents On Children

A negative parenthood style can be mischievous to a child's development and geste. Children who are victims of bad parenthood are two times more likely to come to society.

1. Language

Couples may show discourteousness to each other or others by using crude language. They may frequently curse in front of their children. A child may learn how to swear just by imitating his parents(1).

2. Bad Habits
The bad habits of parents similar to drinking, smoking, and lying can grossly affect the physical and internal health of a child. A child who sees his parents following a chastened life like healthy eating and regular exercising is more likely to imbibe and exercise himself(2).

3. Relationship Issues
Pressure and quarrel between hubby and woman
can mar a child's physical and internal well-being (3). The hostile atmosphere at home will suppress the little bones'
confidence and solicitations. It not only takes a risk on his equation with his parents but may also lead to his dubitation
and mistrust towards connections in general.

4. Temper
Children are frequently the victims of their parents ' bad temper. similar children are likely to develop an unpredictable disposition.

Positive Influence Of Parents On Children
There are colorful positive parenthood styles, which can encourage a child to develop healthy habits and good geste . The parenthood style includes clear and reasonable prospects as well as regardful and probative relations.

1. Clear Communication
Parents need to communicate easily the dos and don'ts to their children. For illustration If you want your child to clean up the room, say, " Please clean- up the room " rather than " Don't make a mess. " A clear communication of praise can give apt provocation to your child.

2. Be A Good part Model
According to Mac Bledsoe, the author of Parenting with quality, being a good part model for the children inspires them to bear better.

rather than using the " Do as I say, not as I do " system, imbibe good rates in yourselves. Flashback parents are a child's first preceptors.

3. Understand Your Child

Gary Smalley, the author of the Homes of Honor Parenting Manual, encourages parents to understand their children's personality types and also conform to their commerce. He insists that parents should appreciate their children with a clinch or a ruffle in the hair once they do the task. Non-verbal communication too can enhance the understanding parents partake with their youthful bones

.

The influence of parents on a child stays for life. Therefore, parents should work on positive influences to inculcate healthy habits and good geste in their children. To do that, parents should avoid negative influences like discourteous geste with others, using crude and vituperative language, and lying.

Rather, parents should understand their child's requirements, communicate with children easily, and act responsibly to lead by illustration. Flashback, parenthood is a responsible job that requires patient sweat. So, keep working on yourself to be the stylish role model for your child.

Chapter 2 : How to train an entitled adult child

Adult Children — When to Help and When to Let Them Learn
Knowing When to Help Adult Children
We've a standing joke in our home when I was working toward a doctoral degree, my sons sometimes started spending plutocrats in their heads. In other words, they liked to plan what they were going to do with the plutocrat I was going to make. I always tell them that I'm leaving all my plutocrats to the dolphins, so they will have to make their way in the world.

On some positions, like all jokes, there's some variety to what I say. I anticipate them to have jobs, work hard, and support themselves in life. The expression" tough love" comes to mind, but as a council psychology professor, family counselor, and former particular loan pen, I've met numerous parents who spent their life savings bailing their children out of predicaments. This composition is for those parents.

The first thing to do is figure out the difference between help that will profit and help that will only hurt your kiddies. Below, you will find sections that answer these main questions

What can you do when your grown kids are making bad opinions and end up in trouble — romantically, financially, emotionally, or with the law?
How can you help your adult child come financially independent?
When is it time to cut the apron strings and close your checkbook?
When is it okay to stop by and help?

When Your overgrown sprat Makes Bad opinions

There's a big difference between trying to fix your adult child's ongoing, tone-created problems and helping a sprat face a life extremity. An adult child who makes a poor decision — like a son who buys a Trainer bag rather than paying her bills, or a son who gambles with his rent plutocrat — should learn from that decision. But also there are real family heads — bus accidents, ails, layoffs, house fires, the list goes on — when families should work together.

When Your Adult Child Does Not hear Your Good Advice

You are saying all the right things to your adult child, but for some reason, they just do not hear. What can you do? Well, the answer depends on whether or not you're supporting your child financially.

Still, also you are not entitled to give them advice unless they ask for it or to try to help a serious mistake If you are not giving them plutocrat. This will allow you to save your breath for when the advice might be heard and make a difference.

Also, you still have a say-so in how their time and plutocracy are spent, If you're financially supporting your adult child. Spend that plutocrat and advice wisely. For illustration, if you want your child to go to council, also offer to continue funding them while they do so(and if you do not want them to drop out of the council, also make it clear that your fiscal support will end if they do not attend).

So unless you are paying the bills, you do not get any say-so in how your adult child conducts their life.

What to Do When an Adult Child Calls From Jail

You get a call at 1 a.m. that your adult child is in jail. After hearing the sob story about scrupulous driving, medicine possession, or some other involvement in illegal exertion, numerous parents will rush to bail their child out of jail. numerous parents go as far as taking out loans to get adult children out of jail. Why? A friend of mine constantly pawned his vehicles to keep his son out of jail for possession of an illegal substance. Indeed though he knows he's enabling this child, he refuses to stop and let his son feel the consequences of his conduct.

In our family, I've made it clear that if one of my children does commodities illegally, they should not call me. They know I'll not bail them out.

Your child is a grown-up. They should be responsible for their actions. However, you're tutoring them that you'll always be there to fix their problems and willingly suffer for their miscalculations If you bail them out of jail and put yourself in fiscal dire woe.

There's another veritably good reason to NOT hock the ranch for bail chances are that adult child is going to continue the geste
that put them in jail. They swear it'll noway be again, and you want to believe. Every parent wants to believe the stylish about their child, but it's your job to know the difference between fantasy and reality.

still, you can be a light and an illustration, but don't save them from the consequences, If your child is headed down a dark path. guarding a child against their miscalculations means that you don't suppose they can handle the situation on their own. However, also you need to admit how you shared in creating the problem If that's what you believe.

As for children who are still dependent, it's important to be clear on whether you're supporting or enabling them.

What to Do When an Adult Child Asks for plutocrat
Numerous youthful grown-ups moment feel to have the idea that mama and pater
are made of plutocrats, so they can spend carelessly. This is the child who gets a new tattoo or a new phone, splurges on a fancy part for a vehicle, buys new clothes, purchases frivolous particulars for their apartment(or worse — gets a brand new vehicle), and also asks you to pay their rent.

Literacy to handle plutocrats in Norway killed anyone. However, it'll only hurt her credit, If your son's vehicle gets repossessed because she can not pay. This type of assignment is important. However, they will never learn how plutocrats work, and they will continue to lean on you for help If you cover your children with these assignments.

34

Too many parents predicate their connections with their kiddies on plutocrat, out of fear that if they don't, their child won't have anything to do with them. That's right, your conduct isn't driven by love but by fear. This is a trap for everyone involved. However, you need not worry about your adult children's Norway calling If you have been a good and loving parent. As they grow up, they will drift down for short spells. This is a natural part of getting grown-ups. They will call, and you'll have great exchanges about their kiddies and life.

Questions to Ask Before You Give plutocrat to Your Adult Child

Ask yourself Can I go? This should always be your first consideration. However, you might want to help them out, also continue to question# 2, If you have the plenitude of a plutocrat. But if you can not go to help them without damage to your fiscal health, also just say no.

Ask yourself Will this plutocrat help? Is this a short-term extremity or a habitual condition? Is it a temporary or an endless need? If your fiscal backing will break the problem now, also move on to question# 3, but if it will not, consider helping them find other results.

Ask yourself Will this plutocrat be used responsibly? Will help pay for commodities important or will it be used on frivolous particulars? Is it for the commodity they need or do they just want it? Is your child following a budget? If your help won't be spent responsibly, also do not give it.

Ask yourself: Is there a commodity I could do to help? occasionally, you can offer another kind of help rather than giving plutocrats. Perhaps you can offer to watch your grandkids while your adult child looks for a job.

Ask yourself, Will it help them gain unborn independence? Some gifts are well spent. Investments in incubating education and backing business gambles are smarter than helping your child take a nice holiday , no matter how desperately that holiday is demanded.

Ask yourself: Is this a pattern? If you have gotten into a habit of funding your adult child, or if you may indeed flatter yourself by continuing to pay for them, it's presumably not healthy or sustainable. It may be time for both you and your adult child to grow up, break the cycle of dependence, and find other ways to maintain your relationship.

Ask your adult child Is this a gift or is it a loan? Both of you must get your prospects straight. You may anticipate being repaid while your adult child is intimately hoping you will forget all about it. Translucency is crucial.

Ask your sprat When will you pay me back? Part of being a grown-up is keeping pledges. bandy a prepayment schedule and make plans for what will be if those dates are broken.

Ask your sprat Are you going to ask me for plutocrat again? Do not get into an implied ongoing fiscal agreement. Have unequivocal conversations about your fiscal prospects.

Note If you want your partner to stop asking you for handouts, the biggest mistake is to say" no" and also let them gripe and cry and guilt you into it. This is precisely why people play niche machines there is always a chance it'll pay off! More to say" no" and stick to it. Saying" no" easily and forcefully is occasionally the stylish thing you can do for your child.

" Arising majority" Happens Between periods 18- 30

Pew Research conducted a recent study that set up that nearly a quarter of 25-34-year-olds are still living with their parents.

But What if Parents Have the plutocrat to Help?
What happens when you have a plutocrat and your children norway have to work for anything? They come useless, unable, entitled grown-ups who have no conception of real work. When a fat, enabling parent dies, their kiddies waste their heritage on stupid effects until it's gone and also they've no idea how to serve.

Part of being a grown-up is paying your way in life. Let your children have their dreams and let them work to negotiate them. Make your children work for commodities. When you help your child from working, they also learn to make it on their own. Let them help the homeless and do charity work indeed if- especially if- you have a plutocrat.

Why Should not a Parent Help Their Child Financially?

When a person works hard for a commodity, they appreciate it, but when a commodity is given, they don't feel a sense of responsibility for it. This is indeed true with the council, where I presently educate. The utmost of the scholars who work hard in part-time jobs and for literacy will appreciate their education, whereas those whose parents pay for their academy are much more likely to drop out.

Some parents say they want their children to have effects easier than they had. Well, why would you want that when you turned out so well? Children need to witness rigors, they need to know the world isn't fair, and occasionally life sucks. Why?

Until you know the pain you don't appreciate health,

until you know poverty you can't appreciate wealth,

until you know failure you can't appreciate an accomplishment,

and until you work for a commodity you can't take pride in retaining it.

Don't burglarize your kiddies. Be there for them with love and moral support, not to fix their miscalculations and/ or hand them your checkbook
These days, the biggest peril facing retirees, the one thing they have not planned for, is having to support adult children and grandchildren.

How You Can Help an Adult Child Without Spoiling Them
When your adult child calls with a problem, talk them through it. bandy their coffers and options.
support your child's intelligence with affirming statements similar as" You're smart, and I am sure you'll figure this out," or" You're strong enough to handle this."
Help them suppose logically. Let them decide what their stylish option is grounded on the coffers available.
It's tempting to shoot plutocrats. Who does not want to help the people around them? But you aren't then to fix the lives of your

children, you're then to educate them to stand on their own and suppose for themselves.

What if You Always Help Them?

When an adult child is dependent, it creates a negative relationship between the child and the parent. The child resents the parent rather than esteem the parent. However, you might start to begrudge them as well, If you had to calculate someone differently for everything. The adult child starts to anticipate the parent to fix their life, therefore creating stress for the parent. Ultimately, life situations buckle from this script.

Case in point

A senior couple is presently in a court battle with the hubby's adult children who want half of everything the man worked for during his life. These adult children are trying to take their heritage before their father has passed away. All their lives their father has given them everything, now they believe they're entitled to further. The man is having to fight an expensive legal battle to keep his plutocrat. There is a fine but pivotal line between parenthood and over-parenting.

Grown-ups Who Still Act Like Children

When Does a Child Come into an Adult?

When is it time to cut the strings, close your checkbook, and back down? Take all of these effects into account when you decide exactly when your child should transition from child to adult

There are numerous different prospects, not only across societies but from one family to the coming. Every family has its own culture which influences every family member's prospects. In some families, multiple generations all pitch in to live under one roof — in others, kiddies are anticipated to move out at 18 to start their own families. So there's no universal cut-off age. You will have to look at your family's unequivocal and implicit hypotheticals and patterns for guidance.

Another thing to consider is the changing times. We used to consider all 18- time- pasts grown-up, but lately, a new term has been added to our vocabulary for what happens between scale from the high academy and eventual independence" Arising majority" is what we now call that transition period between 18- 30.

Pew Research conducted a recent study that set up that nearly a quarter of 25-34-year-olds are still living with their parents.

" Failing to launch" is another new term that describes the incapability of millions of youthful people — indeed those with jobs — to completely transition into independent grown-ups.

Due to a delicate profitable climate(the adding cost of education, the stagnant minimum pay envelope, etc.) we have a growing problem in which numerous youthful people are having a hard time gaining the tone- adequacy of the majority.

What Kind of Help Is Helpful?

When You Should Help Your Adult Child

The utmost adult children will move back home with you at least formally. generally, this happens after the council. By that time, the spouse should be carrying as a roommate rather than a child — cooking, cleaning, doing chores, and contributing to the ménage.

Our deal with our kiddies was they got one time after scale before they had to start paying rent to us. At that time, they were also anticipated to save plutocrats for an apartment and an auto. I would noway let my children starve but, short of that, all life experience(easy and hard) is for their good.

Still, also, of course, you will need to have other plans in place and will need to make arrangements for after you die. If for any reason your kiddies need endless backing(like if they have a disability or a habitual illness) and if you're their only means of support. A fiscal council might suggest smarter ways for you to help in a way that does not qualify them for social services.

Let your adult child live their own life. Don't try to save them. Let them save themselves. I guarantee when your children are old, they will appreciate the values you tutored them and be better people.

The question I have is a twenty- eight- time-old son. He has been clean and sober six times. He lives at home and hasn't worked five times. He's depressed but will not get help. It's veritably sad. As his parents, I agonize. How can I help?

The answer I would start by giving him a reason to work, similar to" starting the coming month you'll be paying$ 450 a month in rent." No matter who I'm talking to, if they aren't engaged in physical exertion(working out) or a sport, they should be. Exercise is a stylish cure for depression, it ups the serotonin situation in the brain. While this does not work for everyone, it does work for the utmost people. Sun is also useful for depression. numerous people who were career medicine addicts crash into depression when they're sober. It's the incapability to deal with life's challenges that goad the medicine use, to begin with. At 28 he has the utmost of his life ahead of him, it's time to live again. However, start taking him hiking, tell him you want to go but do not want to go alone If you're in good physical condition. Get him moving.

Question: My 42- time-old son is homeless living on my property on a roof. I have tried to help him numerous times but can't. Should I just let all the solicitude and anxiety go?

Answer: Is having anxiety and fussing fixing the problem? If it's fixing the problem also by all means continue to feel that way. If it's not fixing the problem also it may be time to get a new perspective. Your son is 42, roof living is his choice. Perhaps you should just accept his choice, let him know that you accept his choice. Also, stop fussing, let him do his own thing.

The question I have an eighteen-time-old son who has been in and out of jail since age 15. Our son was espoused from foster care at age two and diagnosed with fetal alcohol goods. He's now in jail again and is looking at a 2- 7 time captivity judgment. How do you help the sprat who does not learn from his miscalculations? We've Norway bailed him out before, but this time I want to. How do I help him get a fair trial?

Answer: Ask yourself what he's going to do when you bail him out of this mess? Is he going to walk the line or do medicine again? You can get him an attorney but chances are he'll end up back in captivity, and you'll have wasted your plutocrat. Love your son, but realize that this is who he is. This is the life he has chosen for himself. You can be probative without financial compensation. Unless you believe he's fully innocent, I would leave it alone.

Question: We have a 19-time-old son who's veritably willful, norway listens, moved out 3x and came back, failed her first time in university, took a semester break, and works part-time. She spends her plutocrat towards her swain, eats out a lot, and pays a lot on salon care. She paid for her education and a little share in the house. You can not have a good discussion with her because she's always in protective mode. She hovered to move out again, and my hubby said to go ahead. She was resentful because we did not help her pay for her education. What shall we do?

Answer: Everything you mentioned is part of growing up. As long as your son is in the academy and working, let her do what she wants with her plutocrat. Just do not give her a fresh plutocrat when she asks. You do not have to micromanage your son. The assignments will come when she can no longer support her life. If she is not going back to the academy, also charge her rent. However, she moves out, If she moves out. I would educate her to budget, however. This is not a" parents being mean" assignment. This is an" I love you" and this will come in handy.

The question: I've 2 overgrown daughters who both have council degrees. They do not look for work, party all night, or watch television, and also sleep all day. My woman
is a recovering alcoholic, and I also have 2 young daughters who I all have to look after. What should I do as they're using my woman as a guard for their shiftlessness and manipulative geste?

Answer: You're going to have a sit down with your woman and talk about your daughters' geste. You're going to have to get her to agree that this geste can not go on and commodity needs to be done. That commodity is going to be putting your adult daughters under contract to live in your house.

However, paying you rent, moving out in six months, If they don't want to subscribe to the contract and agree to your rules is similar to getting a job. However, get some boxes to pack their stuff and protest them out If they stay and aren't holding up their end of the contract. Indeed adult children want to be parented. Be a parent, not a jellyfish.

Question: My son is twenty- six- times old, living at home, and CPS just took her three-time-old. She's on the wrong path, and I've been holding her hand every step of the way. Lately, it has started to be a serious problem for my hubby and me. How do I help her grow up?

Answer If she's on medicines, get her into a treatment installation. For a lot of youthful women having a baby will make them more responsible. In your son's case, that didn't be. To have CPS take a child, that parent has to be visibly unfit. CSP generally requires parenthood classes. Know that you can not make her a better person, she has to do that on her own. You might want to back off her for a bit. However, she also has no reason to grow up and handle them herself If you're always fixing her problems. Put it to her like this," If she does not take care of her child, why should you take care of her?" She's an adult. However, she should be supporting herself with a job, paying you rent, and taking care of her child, If she's going to stay with you. However, also all you're doing is helping her be reckless If she isn't going to do those effects.

Question: My son is twenty- six- times old and has a job. He takes one council course per semester, and he's an overall night on the computer or television, so he sleeps all day. My hubby says," you can not help him if he does not ask for help." I was bothered, and do not know what to do. How do I help him?

Answer: At one class per semester, he should graduate about sixty times. Why is he not working or paying rent? Your son is not progressing because he does not have positive resistance. You do not have to be mean to him, but he should have been out of your house a long time ago. However, that is up to you, If the two of you're ok with him staying. He could be working part-time and saving plutocrats for his place. The normal rule is if you aren't a full-time pupil, also your work. The two of you aren't helping him by allowing him to voyage. Time to talk, he should be paying rent to stay there, and he should have chores, if he does not want to do that he can get a job and save a plutocrat so he can move out.

Question: My son is 33 and lives on his own, but I've helped him out so much with plutocrats, etc. He will not get up some days to go to work because he says he does not hear the alarm timepiece, so I'll call for 30 twinkles or longer to wake him up. I've paid to have his lights put back on; this has gone for a long time. I've been stressed to the maximum. Every time, I say I am not doing it again. Please give me some ways for me to stop and let me know he'll be OK. What do I need to do?

Answer: Get him a loud alarm timepiece, have him put it across the room so he has to get up to turn it off. Let him fix his miscalculations and figure out his own life. That does not mean you do not love him. It means he's a man that you're treating like a 10-time-old boy. How can he act like a man if you contend with treating him this way? If he gets into trouble, say" You're a man now, you can fix it." He has to get it together on his own. You are not helping him; you're enabling him. Anticipate more, anticipate him to be a man.

The question I am trying not to be a horse, but I realized I'm not trusting my adult children to make opinions. I pry into their lives and am constantly asking them what they plan to do despite them being 29, 31, and 33 times old. They do not ask for a plutocrat, they live on their own, and they all have jobs, but they aren't living up to their eventuality. Two are in the eatery business, and one has a full-time job with benefits. I see them wasting their lives. Do you have suggestions for books that deal with unmotivated grown-ups?

Answer: We give our children life, but it is not our job to tell them how to use it. Happiness isn't resting on fulfilling a parent's idea of our eventuality. Your children aren't asking you for anything; leave them alone. A person can have all the eventuality in the world, but that does not mean they want to come what you suppose they should come.

Consider all those sports daddies who pushed their kiddies to be athletes when the sport did not want to play. Your script is not any different. Why do not you find out what your kiddies' dreams are and support those? I would rather my child pursue a commodity they love that makes them happy than to have them do what I suppose they should do and be miserable. rather than working on your kiddies, look for particular growth openings for yourself. Live by illustration.

Question When you have an adult son who has been arrested and is in jail calling you and soliciting for you to bail him out and making pledge after pledge to noway use medicines again and that he has learned his assignment, how do you stay strong and not feel so shamefaced for not bailing him out?

Answer Well is this his first time in jail? For people who are truly uncurled out of jail, it only takes one time for them to change their ways. However, this person is giving you lip service to get out, If this is the alternate or third time. I am not sure why parents all feel it's necessary to bail these kiddies out. Parents should only feel shamefaced if they were involved.

Question: My 19- time-old son has wrathfulness and internal health issues. I worry about him constantly. He and my hubby don't get on. He can not stay at our home. I can't go financially and help him pay for a home. I love him so much and have tried numerous times to help him with his issues, with support and croakers. My hubby won't let him stay in the house, and I'm ready to end my marriage to go and rent a place for him and me. What should I do?

The answer is I am not sure what you mean by wrathfulnessissues. However, you also need to get him into an installation If your son is mentally unstable. At 19, a lot of youthful men witness truthfulness without cause. The brain does not stop growing until around the age of 25. Our first responsibility in life is to our children, still, once they hit a certain age, they need to be on their own. However, he needs to get a job, and go to council or a trading academy, If his son graduates from high school. However, he is not going to be around much, If your son is working and going to school.

However, you also need to do it without consideration for your son If you want a divorce. Don't use your son or give your son that kind of power. Getting disassociated should norway be because your adult child does not like your partner. Your adult child did not marry your partner, you did.

However, that's one thing; if you just want a reason to leave, that's an additional commodity entirely, If your relationship isn't working. Take responsibility for your passions. Your son isn't going to always be around unless you want to support him. That means you aren't taking care of your relationship with your hubby. I do not understand why you would take the side of your son who's acting out over the hubby who just wants peace in his home.

Question: My 21- time-old son wants to move in with her swain. She still has three semesters of the council left. However, am I right to say you need to get your auto not take mine? Right now we pay her auto insurance, and medical insurance, If she chooses to move out. Should we still pay her charges?
The answer is I'm not sure why she'd suppose you're going to pay her way if she moves out. The point of moving out is taking responsibility for yourself. The only reason you would pay anything is if you promised to help with council charges. As for the auto, it's your auto. There again I'm not sure why she'd suppose taking your auto was an option. We did help our kiddies get their first auto, they were each used vehicles, nothing fancy. substantially bought a private party. All of them had to pay us back for the auto. Encourage independence in your adult child. This is about chastising them because they won't live their life the way you want, it's about giving them the tools they need to succeed in life.

Question: My 29-time-old son has moved back home and now stays out till the early morning hours. I feel like I'm living with a 16 year old and can't take it. What should I do? I also have a senior mama who lives with me too.
Answer Time to set boundaries with your son.

1. Curfew
2. Rent

3. Chores
4. Time limit on staying(I generally say six months)

This is your home, if she can not follow the rules, she cant stay.
Question: My 37- time- wedded son(3 kiddies and pregnant) has always made her life harder than it has to be! It kills me to see her keep running in front of that train. How do I let go? It's a selfish trip

as I've trouble living a happy life knowing she's" suffering." Will she ever learn, and how do I let go?

Answer To overcome any situation in life, a person has to learn new chops. Whatever chops your son presently employs, those chops aren't helping her fix her problems or make better opinions. Also, she's 37 and married; her problems are her problems. Yes, she's choosing the hard road, but it's her choice. Your son is still alive indeed though she has made these opinions; don't save her from her miscalculations presently. Let her be a grown-up.

Question: My 24- time-old son lives under the highway. She left the house because she refuses to live with my hubby who's her stepfather. He was verbally, mentally, and emotionally vituperative to her. She swears to her family that she hasn't been doing medicines or drinking for a while now. I'm planning on leaving my hubby to help her. She also thinks she has PTSD. Am I doing the right thing?

The answer to your question depends on what you want. If you're wedded to a vituperative person also yes you should leave. However, also you should help her, If your hubby meddled with your son with his geste

As for her tone- opinion of PTSD, that needs to be determined by a professional. She may have issues from the abuse, but that does not inescapably mean it's PTSD. The type of help she'll need is a good therapist. However, also I would advise you about the type of help you give her If she has done medicines and abused alcohol in her history. You can pay to have her medicine tested. However, I would say she's still using If she refuses to do it. At that point, the help should be rehab and comforting.

Question: Should I protest my forty-time-old son and five kiddies out of the house? They've destroyed it, and my son is hardly at home. I'm constantly doing her job with my grandkids, and I'm tired.

The answer: I suppose it's time to sit down and bandy her plan for moving out and paying for damages. However, she should be saving to move out, If she has been living with you rent-free. It sounds like you have come to the sitter for your grandchildren. Have her sign a contract that she'll pay rent, pay for the following damages, and be out of your house in six months.

Question: My new hubby and I want to help my alcoholic, 28- time-old, homeless son to move into our new house so she can help babysit her 4- time-old son. She refuses recovery, wrathful operation classes, and tone-medicates with marijuana which helps her mood swings. What's the stylish way we can help our son recover, come responsible, find a job and save for a place of her own as well as recapture guardianship of her son?

Answer: What you're planning to do is set yourself and your son up to fail. However, your life is going to come into a circus of enabling her on a diurnal base, If you move your son in without getting her clean. She doesn't want to help herself if she refuses all the effects you described. The only situation you're fixing by moving her in is that she will not be homeless. Do you want her to get the act together? Allow her to visit and allow her to shower for job interviews.

However, bear with her to stop drinking, If she wants back in your home. However, also she's not ready to change If she gets frenetic and will not stop. You can not make her change. You can stop enabling the geste

. Also, anyone who needs a wrathful operation shouldn't be around a child unsupervised. One day your son may lament this time in her life, she may unbend out. the moment isn't that day. Until also, you have the option to stop awarding her extreme geste

.

Question: My son recently graduated council, and he is moving to Ohio. Should I go with him to show support, or let him go it alone? I feel shamefaced for not going with him to a new place.

Answer: You should go only if he asks you to go. else just tell him how proud you're and move on.

Question: My son was espoused at the age of six due to my dependence. He's 19. He regressed and got caught. Well, he posted a commodity on Snapchat about an elatedness dealer, and I told his espoused mama. He also texted me verbally abusing me and calling me names. My question is, he's graduating Sunday, and I allowed that I don't want to go. I feel it's important to set that boundary so that he can not treat me like that. Am I wrong for not going?

Answer This question is about what you'll lament further. Will you lament not being at the scale? kiddies say effects to their parents in wrathfulness. Considering your particular history with this child it's not surprising. Indeed if you don't talk to him, you should go to the scale.

Question: What should I do when an adult child will not take responsibility?

Answer This is vague, so my answer may be vague. Responsibility is an internal station about our conduct. When people do not take responsibility, it's frequently because they don't want to defy the part of them that makes miscalculations and is wrong. We educate kiddies as they grow up that making miscalculations is bad, yet numerous of us grow from our miscalculations. tutoring someone whose miscalculations are an occasion for growth can change their perspective. Since we all make miscalculations, we can empathize rather than charge and educate rather than sermonize.

Question: My adult son moved home six times ago, but my hubby does not accept rent from her or payments for serviceability. She meddled up her T- score test for acceptance into a nursing program. She works two jobs but refuses to move out of our house because she's hysterical about being alone. What should I do?

Answer: The TEAS score test can be taken twice a year. However, she should also be studying for the test, If she wants to enter a nursing program. Some people hit a stumbling block in their plan and just quit an idea. However, she needs to study and retake the test, If she wants to be a nanny. As for being in your home six times, by now she should have the plutocrat for the down payment on a house.

The problem you have isn't here; it's your hubby. You need to get him on board with the idea of her moving out. Once he's on board, you sit her down, and she has six months to save the plutocrat to move out. She needs to go live her own life. It's time.

Question Our eighteen- time-old son moved out last month because she doesn't want to live with the house rules and has a new swain.

She rents a room with her stylish friend whose father only charges her a couple of hundred bones
a month. She was approved for a government pupil loan and is now spending out-of-control for her swain's gas, allowance, and food. She now wants to introduce him to us. We tutored her to save when she was youthful. What shall we do?

Answer: Meet her swain. Your son is out on her own for the first time. That situation comes with a literacy wind. The effects you tutored her will protest, or she'll learn. There's nothing for you to do except keep a relationship with her. However, meet him, If she wants you to meet the swain. I wouldn't make a big deal out of it. Her spending isn't your problem at this point. You need to let her decide who she's without hindrance. Hopefully, the swain is a good person.

Chapter 3 How to connect with a complicated adult child

It can be hard to accept when your children become overgrown-ups. You spent time taking care of them, furnishing them, and guarding them. Also, you look up one day and they are graduating council and getting wedded.
It's hard to know how to stop enabling overgrown children and what changes are demanded in your parent-child relationship so they can continue to thrive as grown-ups. In this composition, we'll define enabling, why it's dangerous, and how to stop it.

Enabling Your Children May Be Holding Them Back
Why Is Enabling a Bad Thing?

You may have heard you should not enable your adult children. But why? What is so wrong with helping your kiddies? Well, when you enable your child well into the majority, you may suppose you are helping them, but you are holding them back. It may not be purposeful. You just want to make life easier for them so they can be successful.

But it's important to understand the difference between helping and enabling. Then are some signs that you are enabling your child

They live at home, or you pay for their living charges.
You are constantly helping them through their heads.
You constantly make offerings so they can have what they want.
You are overwhelmed by helping your grown child.
You are constantly upset about doing commodities that will hurt or upset them.
A Lot of Parents Are in This Situation

All parents want what is stylish for their children throughout their continuance. It's normal to want to shield them from rigor. Still, at some point, those children grow older and become grown-ups. It may be hard to accept that your children should now be making their own life choices and opinions. It may be hard to see them as anything but that small little sprat that demanded their mammy and daddy for everything.

It may be indeed harder knowing that ultimately they may witness some type of trouble, and you may not be suitable to help. So numerous parents tend to take care of anything within their control, not knowing that they may be precluding their children from growing into responsible grown-ups that can handle their problems. Enabling is more common than you may realize.
There are a large number of adult children continuing to live at home. Learning to move from enabling to empowering your grown children will help them more in the long run. With many simple changes, you can put your adult children on a better path.

What Is Enabling?

In the remedial world, an enabler is someone who habitually allows a family member or close friend to make choices that can affect them in detriment.

Enabling children

You frequently hear of a partner or other loved bones
enabling an addict by justifying their operation or furnishing them with the substances. An enabler feels as though they're helpful at the moment by keeping that other person comfortable and not allowing them to come worried. Still, they are only making effects worse in the long run.

Why Is It dangerous?

Numerous parents have a hard time when their children are coming of age. They do not want them to go out into the cold-wave, dangerous world. So these parents handle a lot of the tasks their adult children should be doing on their own, similar to laundry, cleaning, paying bills, etc. In doing this, their adult children come more comfortable and may stay at home longer since their lives are being taken care of.

Similar parents may find that as the adult child ages, they are ill-equipped to handle the world around them. At some point, whether at 18 or 30, they will enter the real world. However, they are likely to have a hard time performing, If they have been shielded from it. However, cuisine, and cleaning, If their mothers have always done their laundry. They may not know how to write a check or balance their bank account. They may not know how to go grocery shopping or indeed understand a form.

Numerous parents who tend to be unable to forget that their job is to help their children gain life chops. What they need to realize is that they're raising a member of a community, an unborn hand, and presumably someone's unborn partner. It does society an injustice to abstain from tutoring children's independence.

Adult children tend to accept the help they admit, but it's been set up that offering too important help negatively affects the parents. According to a study published in the Journal of Marriage and Family," Parents who perceived their grown children as demanding too important support reported poorer life satisfaction."

How To Change Enabling Actions

51

To correctly enable geste, it's important to understand that geste. It's easy to get lost in the moment of trying to give instant delectation to your child. But now it's time to step back and suppose about the long-term goods of your enabling. suppose about what would be if you tutored your children to do their laundry, cook a mess, or drive. They'd be lost in the world without you. As much as you may want to feel demanded, it's important to not make this about yourself and suppose about your child's future(without your help).

While this may be delicate at first, it's possible. Your adult child may not want to put down their videotape game device to pull their weight in the house because it's been allowed for so long. But it's important to stick to your plan to foster your adult child's independence.

Consider holding a family meeting. bandy motifs similar as

Everyone's places and liabilities.
What you've come to realize about enabling.
What you would like to educate your adult child.
Why do you feel it's important to change the family dynamic?
Helping Yourself

Coming to realize that you may be enabling someone isn't easy. You will probably need support throughout this trip. That is why it's important to calculate your family and musketeers. It may also be salutary to find someone neutral, similar to a therapist. You can find accessible therapists online at BetterHelp. There are hundreds of certified online therapists staying to help.

They may indeed help you discover you've been enabling someone without realizing it. As bandied before, it's veritably delicate for someone to realize they are enabling a person, as they feel as though they're simply helping them.

Helping Them Through It

Your adult children may push back at first. Still, your part as a parent is to see the bigger picture and understand that while they may be happy now, this isn't what is stylish for the long- term.

They may say things like," don't you still love me?" or" why are you so mean to me?" It can be hard losing the support they have grown habituated to. Be understanding and compassionate. But it's important to stay strong enough to hear these studies without changing the course of action. While they may indeed say they do not love you presently, be strong.

This is simply a response to you breaking the cycle. Forced change is uncomfortable, but people only change once they're uncomfortable enough to do so. Another idea is to invite them to a comforting session. numerous youthful grown-ups are on their phones the utmost of the day anyway, so they can plug into an online therapist along with you to do some family work. It may not indeed feel like a remedy to them, but rather texting about life.

Moving Forward

Once you begin to break the cycle of enabling and see your child gain independence, you'll feel overwhelmingly proud of them. It'll make your sweat worthwhile. You will be suitable to see your child make life opinions and choices you would make yourself. You'd be surprised what they can do with a little guidance and a little freedom.

Enabling
Enabling Your Children May Be Holding Them Back
They'll be making you regale and doing your laundry in no time. also, you will be the one
who gets to sit back and play videotape games while they clean around you. Okay, perhaps not relatively, but you'll be suitable to relax knowing that you raised an independent, responsible youthful grown-up who'll do great effects on this world because you let them come themselves.

Making these changes in life might not be easy for you or your child. Having access to online comfort in those tough moments can be the difference between success and failure. Both you and your adult child can reach out for advice. Read reviews on some of BetterHelp's online therapists below.

How to Deal With poisonous Family Dynamics
It's normal to witness an occasional misreading, disagreement, or indeed egoism among family members. Challenges and difficulties aren't that uncommon.

But, if you find that your connections with family members — or indeed just one family member in particular — are especially delicate, you may want to take some time to examine that relationship more closely.

Begin by asking yourself if the relationship is unsafe or just a little awkward to manage. However, you might want to consider limiting your relations with this person, If your family relationship is vituperative.
Exploration shows that prolonged conflict with people as well as negative connections can impact your health

still, on the other hand, you are just dealing with negativity, If. Then there are some tips on managing delicate connections with family.

How to Manage a delicate Relationship
Still, it can help to position the playing field and neutralize some of the difficulties, If you are floundering to navigate a delicate relationship with a family member. Begin by reminding yourself that you have no control over another person's conduct, but you can change your response.

Take some time to think about what you appreciate about your family member, rather than fastening on the effects that make them delicate to be around. When you are together, you'll be less likely to zero in on their faults.

Then are some other tips for effectively managing a delicate relationship.

Suggest meeting someplace neutral. Choosing a position where you both feel at ease can help produce a calmer atmosphere. Meeting in public frequently leads people to be on their stylish geste as utmost do not like to attract attention or make a scene.

Prepare yourself mentally for your interactions. However, it can help to prepare yourself beforehand, If you know you have a gathering coming up where you'll be interacting with delicate family members.

For example, if your aunt regularly criticizes your career choice or makes asleep reflections about your lack of children, suppose how you might respond if that happens. Being prepared ahead of time can help you navigate delicate exchanges and relations with lower stress.

Be compassionate. The most delicate people are not born that way. rather, they came delicately grounded on their life gusts. For example, if your family member has lived a particularly hard life, they may be floundering with bitterness, resentment, or wrathfulness over what life has dealt them. rather than getting irked by their geste , try to look at the situation empathetically. While this doesn't excuse their bad geste , it clearly will help you keep effects in perspective.

How to Interact With a delicate Family Member

Depending on your family member's issues and hot buttons, communication may be grueling, especially if they're particularly delicate to get along with.

still, manipulation, or bullying, If they're prone to wrathfulness. Just because they're family doesn't mean you're emotionally abused in some way.

Still, if your family member is just delicate to be around or challenging to communicate with, these tips might help your relations go a little more easily.

Strategies for Dealing With Specific Problematic Actions

While it may not feel fair that you have to find ways of dealing with a delicate family member or bone

who hates you, a flashback that you only have control over your geste, fastening on what you can control can make the relationship less inviting.

Strategies to Deal With Domineering Family Members

You might have a family member who always takes over exchanges, butts in on other people's exchanges, or wants to control exactly how, where, and when an event takes place. To deal with a tyrannous or controlling family member, try these strategies

Give them control over commodity specific. For illustration, deciding who'll bring what dish to a potluck. This way, they've some power that does not hurt anyone differently.

Do not get caught up in their falsehoods or apologies; flashback what you know to be true.

In exchanges with the person, remain calm and concentrate on the variety and data.

Strategies to Deal WithOver-Dramatic Family Members

still, slip secrets, make up falsehoods for attention, If your family member loves to gossip about everyone.

Refuse to share in dramatic exchanges by saying," I'm not going to share in this discussion, if you want to talk about commodities differently I'd love to converse with you."

Do not reply. Over-dramatic people are seeking big responses; by replying you're inadvertently buttressing their actions.

Do not try to reason with them or change their mind. You can not explain with someone when they're being illogical, and trying to do so can get you smelled into the drama.

Strategies to Deal With Negative Family Members

Call them Negative Nancy or Negative Ned, these family members are always dimmed and particularly like to point out people's excrescences and miscalculations. Dealing with a negative person involves understanding that the problem is theirs, not yours.

Be yourself. However, do not be negative, If you are not a negative person. indeed when they are.

Avoid problems- working. Someone who's depressed or always negative won't respond well to your attempts to putatively" fix" them.

Do not take it tête-à-tête. Their negativity isn't a representation of you and your life, it's a representation of theirs.

Strategies to Deal With Annoying Family Members

Offensive people are generally seeking attention. Or they might suppose they're intrigued by being loud and annoying. This can be veritably aggravating but there are effects you can do

Plan a moment for them to be the star from the start. However, they may be satisfied enough to calm down a little, If they get everyone's concentrated attention off the club.

Let them know in a nice way when they are too loud or they have gone too far. Annoying people generally do not realize they are indeed doing these effects; the actions could be due to anxiety.

Plan quieter, independent conditioning to lessen your relations, while still spending time together.

Strategies to Deal With Family Members Who Have Mental Health enterprises

From personality diseases to depression and anxiety, dealing with family members flaunting internal health enterprises can be inviting. You might indeed feel torn between having empathy for them while also losing your tolerance or energy. What can be helpful is to

Fete their strengths and concentrate on those.

Understand their geste is presumably not particular or only directed at you.

Avoid exchanges about their internal health unless they are asking you for help.

How to Deal With poisonous Family Members

The description of" poisonous" is a commodity that's" veritably dangerous or bad." To deal with poisonous family members, you need to be suitable to fete that they're poisonous and learn when it's stylish to dissociate.

How to Tell if a Family Member or Family Dynamic Is poisonous

still, especially long-term torture, they're poisonous to your life, If your family member causes you emotional or physical torture. Some of the warning signs a person is a poisonous include that they designedly hurt you frequently, norway apologize for their geste, constantly bear your help indeed if it causes you to lose sleep, miss work, or other important effects

condemn you frequently

Attempt to control all major aspects of your life

Abuse you physically, emotionally, or sexually

How to Handle poisonous Family Members

still, there are some strategies you can try to help minimize your torture

If you are not ready to cut your poisonous family member out of your life.

Decide your relationship boundaries and stick to them. You do not need to partake in what these are with anyone.

Be conscious of what you do share.

Decline assignments if you need to.

Avoid alcohol and medicines during interactions. However, remove them as options for anyone, If possible.

Seek remedies to help you deal with family issues.

How to dissociate From poisonous Family Members

still, empathy, or attempts to be a better person, If your family member is easily poisonous and shows no signs of tone-awareness.However, there are two introductory approaches, If you've decided to dissociate from a poisonous family member.

You can" ghost" them and just cut all ties, change your phone number, and exclude ways for them to get your contact information. This approach is stylish for vituperative connections.

You can tell them you need a break and avoid responding to their attempts to communicate.

still, inform other family members of your decision so it's not a surprise to them If you dissociate from a poisonous family member.

Also, make sure you have support in place for yourself, and take safety preventives if you suppose it's necessary.

Focus on Your Growth

As important as you would like tips and advice to make your relationship more automatic, it does not be overnight. Focus on who you're and what you can do to deal with delicate family members as your ultimate strategy. However, seek help from a professional counselor or therapist, If you feel hopeless or helpless about your family problems.

However, you can explore family remedies, If you suppose your family members would be open to it.

Life is much easier when you have a probative family that sticks with you through thick and thin. Family relationships are important for a person at every stage of life. When life gets hard and starts to grip down from your control, the kind words of your mama, partner or siblings calm your soul and give you the strength and courage to take on life head-on. In this post, we talk about the significance of family, its characteristics, and ways to make a strong relationship with family members.

What Constitutes A Family?
A family constitutes people who are related to each other and partake in an emotional bond and analogous values. Family members can be related by birth, marriage, or relinquishment.

Your immediate family includes parents, siblings, partners, and children. And your extended family includes people you're related to, similar as grandparents, relatives, aunts & uncles, whoresons, whoresons, etc.
Families are of different sizes — nuclear(a couple and their children), joint(a couple, their children, grandchildren), amalgamated(a couple, their children, and children from their former marriages), etc.

Why Are Family Connections Important?
A family is important because our internal growth, well-being, and stability all depend on our family.

A family makes all its members feel safe and connected.
It provides us with the comfort of having people by our side during tough times, helping us to manage our stress.
A family allows us to feel safe, defended, accepted, and loved despite our failings.
Families are the introductory units that educate children about connections. Children brought up in a healthy family will be suitable to form better bonds outside their home.
Strong connections educate us on how to make trust with others as family members partake in both good and bad times together.

Conflicts in the family educate children in a regardful way to resolve problems in the future.

A strong family is all a person needs to come confident in life.

What Are The Characteristics Of A Strong Family?

Each family is different. But all strong families have some common features. Many of them are listed below

Have good communication. A healthy family addresses and listens to every member. It encourages grown-ups and children likewise to have a say-so in the decision timber, partake their opinions, or talk about their prospects and bummers.

Partake a feeling of togetherness. The members of the family share common beliefs and, thus, feel connected to each other. This sense of similarity yields cerebral protestation and bone

has the satisfaction of being together with like-inclined people.

Spend time with each other. They make sure to have at least one mess together every day. They enjoy playing, boarding, dining out, or simply agitating politics. They laboriously involve themselves in each other's lives but know where to draw a line.

Show care and affection to every member. The members have kind words to say to each other. They accept you unconditionally but guide you on to the right path if you're swinging. With their care and affection, they make you feel belonged.

Lead by illustration. The elders follow what they educate the young members of the family. The value system is set up by illustration.

Support its members. The world might be against you, but your family is with you. It supports you in your fight, and lets you know they're with you in your opinions. A well-knit family doesn't distinguish between family members and responds to everybody's requirements.

See an extreme situation as an occasion to grow. They strive to see commodity positives in all circumstances, helping you to manage adverse situations without getting overwhelmed.

Focus on every member's well-being. The family members work as a platoon to cover and give to each other. Only the feeling of collective love can motivate people into compromising on their comforts for the happiness of their family.

Show adaptability. Every family goes through ups and downs in their lives and partakes painful experiences together. But no distressing experience loosens the bond. The virtue of fidelity comes from a family.

The flashback that all these merits of a strong family don't come overnight. You need to work together in time to make a healthy family.

How To Make Strong Family connections?
Then are some ways to make strong family connections

1. Spend quality time
Set away some time(perhaps mess times) every day as family time, when you can talk about effects and laugh together.

Share family stories or ask everyday simple things to encourage discussion, similar as " Hey, what did you do in the academy? ", or " How are you changing your new Math schoolteacher? "
Set away one-on-one converse time for everyone in the family to foster your bond. It can simply be five twinkles before going to bed, but this can bring every member close to one another.
Set some time piecemeal simply for your mate.
2. Maintain good communication with everyone in the family
When your children or partner want to talk, admire their needs and hear them with attention. Give them enough time to express themselves duly.

Be approachable to talk about delicate effects. Talking about passions like wrathfulness or frustration or delicate issues should be eating rather than shuffling them. Talking about them doesn't mean you're encouraging them but are helping break the problem. Also, be drinking indeed for uncomfortable exchanges. That's how people make trust that they can go to a family with any issue.
Be ready for a robotic discussion with kiddies. They frequently talk about their passions before going to bed or in the shower. hear them.
Be set to talk about matters of concern, especially with teenagers. Families find it delicate to bandy coitus, alcohol, medicines, or finances with the young members. Still, it's through a discussion that you can address similar matters.

Encourage-verbal discussion through simple gestures like a warm kiss on the forepart every night before your children go to bed. It can bear your love for them.

3. Appreciate everyone in the family

Appreciate every member for performing their duties well. For illustration, praising and thanking a teenager for taking care of a youngish stock will make them feel important.

4. Acknowledge and celebrate each other's bents, differences, and strengths

A good family always cherishes the oneness of each of its members and acknowledges their capacities and strengths. At the same time, they help each other correct their failings.

5. Stay focused on the current problem

Don't bring up former issues every time you have to address a problem. In that way, you can avoid the unpleasantness and rather, concentrate on the issue at hand.

6. Work like a platoon

When your family works as a platoon, every member feels conceded for their donation. Partake ménage chores. Allow little children to share in chores like picking up their toys or putting their shoes back.

7. Establish clear family rules

Make family rules that easily mention how every member should bear and treat each other. For example, " We talk hypocritically with everyone in our family, " or " In our family, we help each other no matter what. ``Similar small but clear rules can make the family stronger and peaceful.

8. Educate children to forgive and make amends

Healthy families educate their members on how to apologize and forgive others when someone makes a mistake. It teaches children to take responsibility for their conduct. Try to have delightful family rituals, which are special to your family, to increase the sense of belongingness.

The first relationship that you establish after birth is with your family. When life seems grueling, your family plays a part in supporting you. Good communication, a feeling of togetherness, and constant support are common features of a tender family.

To establish a stronger bond with your family, spend quality time with them, appreciate their sweats, and work together. People living in loving families have better stations and richer values. Still, creating similar families isn't easy. It requires hard work and fidelity to stay together and achieve a common thing.

Negativity is unhealthy

Studies show that enduring, angry, negative people are frequently unhealthy throughout their lives and die before. According to the Mayo Clinic, they can suffer from high blood pressure, depression, headaches, habitual pain, digestive problems, wakefulness, a weak vulnerable system, and further.

Harboring wrathfulness and resentment, and holding on to hurt and hurt, takes a lot of energy. Your body and your mind have to work harder to accommodate all that negativity, which ultimately causes damage to both your internal and physical health. By forgiving family members, letting go of grievances, and releasing the history, your mind and body can come free and healthy.

Your children need a positive part model

Children look to their parents first as part models. However, your children will grow up with passions of truthfulness and resentment as well, causing difficulties in the academy, If you're enduring cousins and others.

Indeed if you want to spend your life bottled down with passions of wrathfulness, frustration, vengeance, and resentment, you don't want the same thing for your little ones. However, do it for the sake of your children, If you can't let go and forgive family members for your own sake.

remission can make a character

Developing a genuine, strong character happens over your continuance. You develop character by dealing with delicate effects and prostrating them. However, they will tell you the significance of remission and letting go of ill passions, If you've ever talked with people you respect with strong character and integrity. You can't begin to make a positive, strong character if you can't move on from negative aspects of your life.

There are two sides to every story

Still, chances are you believe what happened is all(or substantially) the other person's fault, If you have had a falling out with a family member. Still, there are two sides to every story.

However, chances are he/ she was going through a delicate commodity tête-à-tête, If this person treated you poorly or did something you believed was innocently or fairly wrong. When people act out, it's generally because they're facing challenges that they can't handle. Consider the other side of the story and take a way toward remission.

Life is too short

grievances, arguments, resentment, and truthfulness can make gatherings delicate for everyone. The stress of family rifts can take a risk not only on you but the rest of your cousins as well. When it comes down to it, the biggest reason that you should forgive family members is that life is too short.

Life is transitory, and you know when you're going to lose someone to death. Look at the big picture. Forgive and mend your connections with family. You don't want to be left with regrets once they're gone.

Encourage-verbal discussion through simple gestures like a warm kiss on the foreparts every night before your children go to bed. It can bear your love for them.

Chapter 4 How love and forgiveness connect

Remission: Agitating it as a family

Remission can be delicate to navigate. Learn about ideas for tutoring children and agitating it as a family.

When was the last time you forgave someone for a commodity they said or did? Did it take a long time or just many twinkles? Did it come with a reason? Did you forgive for the good of yourself or your family? Ever wonder what exactly remission is? " remission What's it and how do I do it? " bandied how to define remission, the way of remission, and some of the benefits associated with remission.

Remission can be an important part of relationship growth between two individualities, but also within a group, similar to a family.

Part of creating a strong and healthy family relationship is being suitable to bandy problems or situations that do where remission may be exercised, and for parents that can be a delicate discussion to navigate.

As grown-ups, it can be delicate to navigate the passions and feelings girding remission, so imagine how confusing it can be for children who may not be suitable to name those passions and feelings they're passing. That's why grown-ups need to have some ideas for helping children through remission.

Remission isn't forgetting. Children and numerous grown-ups vacillate to forgive because they believe it means blinking the other person's actions. There's also a misperception that forgiving means forgetting, which might bring on the fear that it'll be again. In reality, to forgive is to say, " I didn't like or appreciate your words or conduct, but I'm willing to let go because it doesn't help me to hold onto these passions. "

To forgive someone, we need to look beyond the action and explore the person. For illustration, if your child is worried Susie called them a bad name during recess, help your child explore what's passing.

Perhaps Susie was on the outskirts of the hop-scotch game and wanted to play. Perhaps Susie felt bad she wasn't invited to play or was jealous of those who were. Helping your child understand a possible detector for the person's conduct encourages compassion and remission.

Before asking your child to let go, forgive or excuse a geste , it's first important to identify the feeling your child is passing. Are they angry, embarrassed, or disappointed? Do they need to understand how the incident made them feel before they can forgive?

State the feeling before offering remission. rather than asking your child to incontinently accept their stock's " I 'm sorry, " have their state how they feel. For illustration, " Jenny, I'm angry you espoused my shirt without asking. Please ask me before taking my time. I forgive you. "

Once the passions are understood, visualization can help your child let go of any harbored passions. Hand your child a pretend balloon. Ask them to suppose about the passions they stated — wrathfulness, sadness, embarrassment. also, ask them to blow all of those passions into the pretend balloon.
Tell them an imaginary string ties the balloon to them. When they're ready to let go of the passions, hand over mock scissors to cut the string and release the passions. Help your child imagine the balloon sailing high into the sky. When ready, imagine the balloon gently popping, spreading a dusting of love and compassion to both parties. Remind your child it might take further than formerly and they can exercise the visualization as much as they would like.

Write a letter. This is a helpful exercise, particularly for teens. Exercise writing a letter stating what caused the worries and how they feel about it. Also, have your child write a compassion statement or one of remission to the lawbreaker and themselves. End the exercise by having them rip the letter up into the scrap, signifying the release of remission.

Be the illustration. Show your child how you forgive others.

Anyhow of which suggestion you try, the key is to communicate. Having an open discussion about remission and the passions or feelings associated with a situation that may need remission is vitally important to erecting a strong family unit.

Why Is It Harder to Forgive Family Members?

remission is norway easy. Being hurt or wronged by someone differently is delicate, and it's mortal nature to feel pain. Yet occasionally, when musketeers, co-workers, or others have wronged you, forgiving them may feel easier than when you have been hurt by a family member. Why is it harder to forgive family members?

Greater Emotional Investment, Greater Pain

The most egregious answer as to why remission is more delicate with family members than with others is that with your family, being hurt is more painful because you have a lesser emotional investment in the relationship.

As families, you may have the anticipation of treating one another stylishly because of the strong emotional and physical ties, yet frequently, you end up hurting each other the most because you develop some position of forbearance or incuriosity given the volume of time spent together.

passing the emotional highs and lows of life with family members binds you together like no other relationship. Yet, it's this veritable bond that makes it much more delicate to forgive each other when there's pain foisted within family connections.

Why It Is further Important to Forgive Family Members

Forgiving family members is more important than forgiving others for the same reasons that family- convinced pain can be more painful family bonds are stronger. A lack of remission can't only weaken those connections, but also maybe indeed destroy them. musketeers will come and go, but connections with your family members are the most important to maintain.

Remission within families has been shown to increase positive family functioning, while a lack of remission does the contrary. consorts who can forgive one another produce better connections not only with each other but also with their children. Your child will manage better with both family and life problems when remission is tutored and rehearsed within the home.

The capability to forgive is particularly mending when there's medicine or alcohol abuse within the family. While remission isn't to be confused with authorization, forgiving one another is crucial in the mending process for not only the individual but also the entire family. While actions during substance abuse are frequently veritably painful for family members, remission, particularly when sought after by the existent, has the power to heal and maybe indeed strengthen family bonds.

Why Should I Forgive My Adolescence?

Parents can be especially hurt when their child abuses substances and indulges in actions that are veritably mischievous and painful to the family.

As parents, you have handed for their emotional and temporal requirements, frequently at great immolation. That your child might bear this way toward you seems not only veritably ungrateful but also incredibly painful.

Still, offering remission for the pain they've caused benefits you the most. Being willing to forgive allows you to be a better parent for them. Forgiving offers some measure of understanding that they, too, are hurting, yet allows you to move forward with structure and boundaries that are fair and helpful for them in their recovery.

Why Teens Need remission utmost of All

Offering remission to teens can be one of the topmost gifts a parent can offer. Giving nice gifts and offering temporal support help a child feel supported, but being willing to offer the olive branch when they've hurt you demonstrates unconditional love.

Telling them " I love you, no matter what " is one thing, but being willing to back that up with genuine remission teaches them that they're truly loved and valued. Demonstrating unconditional love and forgiving your child may feel like the hardest thing you can do, but holding a grudge is more painful for everyone in the long run.

Again, remission isn't authorization to hurt you again. Offering consequences, structure, and support in recovery are part of the remission process. remission means that you don't hold their once conduct against them, while consequences and discipline mean that you love them enough to help them in their recovery process. Adolescents in recovery need love and remission for them to love and forgive themselves and to be suitable to move forward in their own lives.

What if My remission Is Not Accepted?

occasionally when you offer remission, indeed in families, it isn't accepted. That's each existence's right, indeed if it seems ungrateful or cruel. occasionally words or responses you had to a family member's actions may still hurt them, or they're simply not ready or suitable to accept your remission.

Offering your remission without strings attached is harder in families, but also allows you to heal from the pain they caused you. This includes your child, indeed if it may hurt if they don't accept the remission you offer.

Why is it harder to forgive family members? The emotional investment increases the quantum of pain that you feel, particularly when it's your child who hurts you. Still, it's more important to forgive family members, especially teens, for the actions of substance abuse. Your remission can bring them love and mending if accepted, but most importantly, it brings mending to you and makes you a better parent.

Chapter 5: How to have that solid communication and relationship with your adult child

The key to utmost relations with adult children is to act as you would bear if the person weren't related to you. Imagine that you're dealing with a young grown-up with whom you're close, but who isn't a part of your family. It may help you to have a particular person in mind.

When you're considering saying commodities to your adult child, ask yourself," Would I speak this way to Johnny?" If the answer is no, also do not say it, or say it differently. Our family members earn at least the same courtesy that we extend to the world at large.

That is, of course, a good rule for nearly every person in nearly every situation, but it's also delicate for us all. Everyone at some time or another is going to say something he or she shouldn't have said. remission is more likely, still, if we've erected up a history of being kind and interfering.

Do not make statements about how you raised your children
similar statements frequently have an erected- in a critical tone. You're allowed, still, to tell funny stories about how commodities you did as a parent boomerang on you or to relate in a kind of" gee-whiz" manner some of the strange effects parents used to do" Can you believe I bought you a cap gun when you were three?" else, be apprehensive that child-rearing doctrines and practices have changed since you were a youthful parent. Respect that.

Flashback to hear
Half of communicating is composed of the dispatches you shoot out. The other half consists of the dispatches you admit. Some grandparents have trouble with that alternate half. occasionally we are distracted. occasionally we want to jump right in with our ideas or results. rehearsing listening chops can make nearly any relationship healthier and happier.

Love your adult child as well as your grandchild.
Children occasionally humorously complain that once they give us grandchildren, they norway get any attention. It's important to nurture your relationship with your adult children. Make it a point to relate to your child as a grown-up and bandy jobs, pictures, politics, and motifs unconnected to your grandchildren. Do effects with your children that do not involve the grandchildren. Appreciate them as grown-ups.

8 Secrets to Speaking with Adult Children That make Up Your Relationship
Krista's mama was coming for a visit and her stomach was formerly tied in knots. As a child, her mama constantly told her what to do and how to do it. And to eclipse it off, Krista felt she did not do it relatively well enough. Now she was 33 times old, but she still felt like that eight-time-old little girl when mama came to visit.

During one of her visits, her mama said, " Krista, I've some redundant time moments. Would you like for me to rearrange your bookshelves to look better? " What Krista wanted to do was to scream and say, " No! I like them just the way they are! You do your bookshelves the way you like them, and I 'll do mine the way I like them! Leave my stuff alone. " Rather, she just expressed her frustration and said, " No, thank you. "

Brittany's mama was much the same. On one visit, she pulled Brittany into the bedroom and said, " I want to tell you a commodity. " Brittany allowed
it was unusual but was hoping her mama was eventually going to partake commodity meaningful for a change. rather, her mama said, " Brittany, let me show you how to tuck the corners of your wastes in duly. " She began to demonstrate the perfect military crowds. Brittany just stood there. " unthinkable, " she said as she turned and walked out of the door.
I've heard of stories like those while writing the book, The Power of a Woman's Words, but I suppose these are enough to give us a good idea of how to have a bad relationship. My mama was much like Krista's, and indeed though mama has left this earth, I can still feel that knot tied with the cords of frustration in my stomach that came with her visits.

It's Complicated
I've always allowed that responding to someone's question with, " It's complicated, " was a total bobby
- eschewal. It's like saying, " I just don't want to talk about it " or " You could norway understand. " But how to talk to adult children effectively is complicated! There are so numerous variables to consider when talking to these brutes … of which I'm one. Let's look at the five keys to " adult speak. "

Number One A Changing Relationship
When it comes to speaking to an adult child, we should talk to him or her more as we'd to a friend rather than a child. Parents frequently visualize being stylish musketeers with their adult children. And while the relationship may have numerous angles of a great fellowship, there are differences.

We get to choose our musketeers. We don't get to choose our children. And once you've got them, you can't shoot them back for a further compatible model.

A parent invests time, feelings, plutocrat, and energy in a child time after time. Parents are nowhere near as invested in a fellowship as they're with their children. However, we can conclude- out of the relationship, If a friend disappoints or hurts us. Not so with children! Parenting is endless.

As Elizabeth Stone has put it, "Deciding to have a child — it is momentous. It's to decide to have your heart go walking around outside your body. " But at some point, we've to allow that heart to beat on its own.

Number Two Encountering Differences

Most of the time our musketeers are like us. We've analogous interests, opinions, worldviews, and pursuits. Not so with adult children. An adult child may be drastically different from his or her parents with contrary political, social, and moral beliefs. Their pursuits, interests, and pretensions may have no similarities.

An adult child may make life choices that run as opposed to what they were tutored under the parent's roof. At some point, the parents may wonder where in the world this person came from, and who abducted that biddable 10- time-old and replaced him with this bigger, aged, extensively different interpretation. The relational metamorphosis from child to grown-up is like a tadpole morphing into a frog, where the last phase is occasionally unrecognizable from the first

Number Three Admitting Personality

Another factor in decoding the " adult child speak " law is personality differences. A mama can say the same thing to two different adult children and get two different responses. One adult child interprets a mama saying, " Do you want me to help you with your laundry? " as a welcome offer to relieve the pressure of running a home. Another adult child hears that same statement and interprets it as " You're not able to keep up with the housework. I don't like how you're so messy. You need me to stop by and take over. "

I know. It's complicated. Another mama told me about how her four daughters responded to the simple words, " Drive safe, " when they left her house. Three of the girls interpreted her farewell as a loving

" farewell. " The fourth interpreted it as " you don't suppose I'm a good motorist. "

The key is to understand the adult child's tendencies and draft our words precisely. And indeed also, what works in one situation may not work in another.

Number Four Hearing Else

Another piece of the mystification is that boys and girls — rather, men and women — perceive words differently. Stereotypically, men tend to take words at face value while women tend to wonder what you mean. Birth order can also come into play. A straightforward first-born may tend to admit words from the sensitive middle child. Is your head spinning yet?

Number Five Filtering through Past Pain

And eventually, we can't ignore the fact that words are filtered through the sieve of history hurts and hurdles. Did a child experience abandonment or bullying as a child? Did the adolescent experience medicine dependence or sexual abuse? Did the youthful adult experience ruin, rejection, or loss? Indeed as an adult myself, I always ask myself if I'm interpreting others ' words through the sludge of once pain. once guests affect present perception.

occasionally parents come so frustratedly and confused about how to use their words with grown children, that they just give up and float on, letting the words take them where they will. I have got a better idea. While we aren't to use our words to inescapably steer the adult child, we can use our words to steer the relationship between us. Also, if they feel safe and secure enough to ask for direction, we can make suggestions and pull out the chart of wisdom and once experience.

This is a list of eight common tendencies to avoid.

Words that Make Adult Children Want to Run for the Hills(Don't Say It!)

1. Don't tell them how to raise their children. Those precious little bones

are their children, not grandma's.

2. Don't remind them of the way you raised them, similar to " That's not the way I raised you " or " I would have no way let you get down with that. " Believe me, they got it. However, also that's their decision If they choose a different route. This doesn't mean forgetting funny stories about their nonage. My son loves to tell stories about how we raised him, especially the disciplined variety.

3. Don't be rude. Don't allow a family connection to be a reason for rudeness or lack of respect. Talk to your adult child with the respect you would any other grown-up. When speaking to him or her, ask yourself, Would I speak to a friend that way? If not, don't say it, or say it differently.

4. Don't jump in with results and ideas to try to break his or her problems. Rather, be a sounding board and ask good questions. Allow the adult children to come to her results, indeed if you do not suppose it's inescapably the stylish one.

5. It might take every bit of restraint you have in you, but don't advise unless you're asked for it. also reply with, " What I would do … " rather than " what you should do. " We all know that wisdom comes with age. But there's a question to consider: Where did that wisdom come from? I don't know about you, but the utmost of my wisdom came from trial and error, substantially error. Once adult children see that the parent isn't going to give unasked advice, he or they'll be more likely to ask for it.

6. Don't partake in a private discussion that you've had with your adult child with someone different. This is true for any participating confidence, but it's worth emphasizing in parent/ adult child connections.

7. Don't take it tête-à-tête if the adult child doesn't have time for a long, drawn-out discussion on any particular day. Flashback to how busy your life was at that stage of life. And just because mama and pater have retired and have time on their hands doesn't mean that their adult kiddies have time to suddenly fill the void.

8. Don't forget you're a guest in their home. masters- in-law need to flashback, once an adult child gets wedded, there's a new woman in the house … and it's not mama. Whether it's a son taking a woman, or a son taking a hubby, the woman
is now the queen of her castle. The mama or mama-in-law, as well as the father-in-law, is a guest.

9. When adult children call on the phone, don't say, " I was wondering when I was going to hear from you " or " I haven't heard from you in a long time. " Avoid any statement that makes him or her feel shamefaced for not calling earlier.

The nethermost line is that when children transubstantiate into youthful grown-ups, a parent's words need to transubstantiate right along with them. Failure to see and treat the grown child as an adult friend will ruin a relationship, occasionally beyond form. While we aren't to use our words to inescapably steer the adult child, we can use our words to steer the relationship between us.

Improving communication with adult children helps you better navigate the natural ebbs and flows of your relationship as you age.

Tip# 1 Use Your Children's Preferred Communication styles
It has no way been easier to communicate with the people around you. And yet, we frequently find ourselves frustrated when we can't find quality time to talk to our adult children. Of course, you flashback to what it was like to juggle mind for a family, work, and also trying to find time to catch up with your loved bones

.

Make sure that you find out how your adult children prefer to communicate. hear what they say but also observe them over time. Make note of which medium they most readily respond to.
However, we recommend communicating with them on those mediums, If you find they enjoy FaceTime calls or respond more snappily to textbooks or Facebook dispatches than traditional phone calls.

Once you make the birth of communication, you'll find it easier to arrange a phone call and further solid catch-up time. Flashback to your children loving you and wanting you to be a part of their life, indeed if they feel busy and distracted at times. The better you can fit into their diurnal measures, the more successful you'll be at staying in touch!

Still, ask your children to help! Or, connect with a community association in your area – numerous offer introductory classes that can help you learn to text. If you need a little help with the technology, feel more comfortable before jumping in.

Tip# 2 Highlight Common Interests
One of the reasons you may struggle to connect with your adult children is because your interests may vary from theirs. But, we go, you still have many effects in common! Some motifs that may get the discussion started could include TV shows or books you're reading. You could indeed ask them for their recommendations!

maybe you have common pursuits – perhaps you both love creatures or gardening? Or perhaps you're trying out a new exercise authority and your child is a fitness buff with lots of advice to offer!

While it may feel silly at first to engage in what some may consider " small talk, " the verity is that we frequently let down our guard with family and forget their individualities first. In doing so, we may fall into the same old pattern of communication over and over. Before you know it, you don't have anything new or intriguing to bandy about and the discussion booths.

Tip# 3 Be Wise When participating in Your Wisdom
Now that you're happily texting and face-timing your children while engaging them with common interests, it's time for our veritably last tip ….

BE WISE WHEN SHARING YOUR WISDOM.

We live in strange times. So much has changed over the decades and your adult children have different pressures and enterprises than you did. Does that mean you don't have helpful advice and wisdom to partake in? Of course not!

It simply means that to avoid the vicious cycle of immolation advice and also having your passions hurt when it's not appreciated, it's preferable to stay until you're asked. (By the way, we tell them to hear you, too!)

The flashback that the entire purpose of perfecting communication with your adult children is to make trust and nurture your relationship. In doing so, they will seek out your advice naturally as they no longer struggle with the obstacles life throws their way. And you'll find that because you've worked so diligently on your communication in the history, your advice will reverberate with them indeed more.

How to Have a Good Relationship with Your Adult Children
Navigating a relationship with adult children can be tricky. When they were kiddies, you knew what your liabilities were. You handed them introductory requirements similar to food, clothes, and medical care, as well as a safe and probative terrain to grow up in. They reckoned on you for everything.

But what happens when your kiddies come from independent grown-ups who don't need you presently?

Whether they're learning to walk, heading off to their first day of the academy, or moving into their first reimbursement, they'll always be your children. But as your kiddies develop, your relationship needs to develop, too.
There are some tips to acclimatize to your new dynamic and foster a good relationship with your adult children.

Let them go and admire new boundaries
It's normal for grown-ups to pull down from their parents a little to define their identity and make independence. Support your grown kiddies to stand on their bases, and respect this increased need for sequestration.

It may be tempting to call them several times a day or show up at their place unannounced, but a lack of respect for boundaries can damage your relationship.

Letting go can be hard, but it's an essential structure block for a healthy parent-grown-child relationship.

Don't offer advice unless asked
Part of growing up is learning to make your own opinions. You may have had reign over what they wore, ate, and did when they were youngish, but now your kiddies are grown-ups, you'll need to break away from that part.

Avoid the appetite to express your opinion or judgment, as this can be hurtful and drive them down. Let them do effects their way, admire their standpoint, and don't offer any unasked advice.

Give them positive feedback and confirmation
Children want to make their parents proud, indeed when they're all grown up. It's important to celebrate their independence and let them know they're doing a good job.

Positive feedback similar to " your new place looks great " or " I 'm so proud of you for being independent " can give the confirmation that youthful grown-ups need to have confidence.

Find delightful ways to spend time together
When you live together, ' family time ' happens naturally. But when your kiddies grow up, you may need to get creative to spend time together outside of the fortnightly Sunday repast.

Embrace this occasion to form a fellowship with your child, and do the effects you love together. Whether it's cuisine, exercising, watching sport, or going to the cinema, find conditioning to connect and discourse over.

Don't guilt them
Children need independence to succeed, and defying their autonomy or being too emotionally indigent can drive a wedge between you.

Don't guilt them about moving out of home, or not visiting or calling enough. This can make visiting or calling you feel like an obligation or chore. Chances are your adult kiddies are busy with work, connections, and other liabilities. Be realistic about where you fit into your child's life now they're all grown up, and make the utmost of the time you do have together.

Printed in Great Britain
by Amazon

47307418R00046